LINCOLN CHRISTIAN COL

W9-CBU-464

BEYOND THE FRINGE

NICK POLLARD WITH
PAUL HARRIS   PHIL WALL
TONY WATKINS

BEYOND THE FRINGE

REACHING PEOPLE OUTSIDE THE CHURCH

Inter-Varsity Press

INTER-VARSITY PRESS
38 De Montfort Street, Leicester LE1 7GP, England

© Inter-Varsity Press 1999

Nick Pollard, Paul Harris, Tony Watkins and Phil Wall have asserted their right under the Copyright, Designs and Patents Act, 1988, to be identified as Authors of this work.

All rights reserved. No part of this publication may be reproduced, stored in a retrieval system, or transmitted, in any form or by any means, electronic, mechanical, photocopying, recording or otherwise, without the prior permission of the publisher or the Copyright Licensing Agency.

Unless otherwise stated, Scripture quotations are taken from the Holy Bible, New International Version. Copyright ©1973, 1978, 1984 by International Bible Society. First published in Great Britain 1979. Inclusive Language version 1995, 1996. Used by permission of Hodder & Stoughton, a member of the Hodder Headline Group. All rights reserved. 'NIV' is a registered trademark of International Bible Society. UK trademark number 1448790.

First published 1999

British Library Cataloguing in Publication Data
A catalogue record for this book is available from the British Library.

ISBN 0–85111–648–5

Set in Garamond
Typeset in Great Britain
Printed and bound in Great Britain by Caledonian International
Book Manufacturing Ltd, Glasgow

Inter-Varsity Press is the book-publishing division of the Universities and Colleges Christian Fellowship (formerly the Inter-Varsity Fellowship), a student movement linking Christian Unions in universities and colleges throughout Great Britain, and a member movement of the International Fellowship of Evangelical Students. For more information about local and national activities write to UCCF, 38 De Montfort Street, Leicester LE1 7GP.

Dedication

In loving memory of Nick Pollard's brother-in-law Ivor St Jean Dick (17/09/1952 — 04/01/1998). He was as comfortable in the rugby club as he was in the Sunday school. And he was appreciated as much in the Scout hall as he was in the church. He, of all people, knew how to reach out 'beyond the fringe'.

9.46

99345

CONTENTS

Preface

NICK POLLARD

Bridget is thirtysomething. She is bright, creative and successful and has just started a great new job in television production. She spends her evenings eating and drinking with her friends and looks as if she has it all.

But most nights she records in her diary her sense of failure and despair. She is desperate to find a man who will be truly committed to her, instead of just using her and leaving her. She lurches from torrid affair to pregnancy scare. She worries about dying alone and being eaten by an Alsatian. She is convinced that if only she could get down to 8st 7lb, stop smoking and give up Lottery Instants, all would be fine.

Rob is about the same age. Some years ago he dropped out of university and into a dead-end job running a second-hand record shop. He can't keep a girlfriend and life seems hopeless. 'Life is like some film where the money ran out, and there are no sets, or locations, or supporting actors, and it's just one bloke on his own staring into the camera with nothing to do and nobody to speak to.' Like Bridget, he is afraid of dying.

Elizabeth is more scared of living than of dying. 'One morning you wake up afraid you are going to live.' Like Bridget, Elizabeth parties and drinks a lot. She also takes a lot of drugs. But none of these can relieve her feeling of hopelessness and depression. 'No-one will ever love me. I will live and die alone.'

Bridget, Rob and Elizabeth are not unusual. They are typical of many in today's generation. In fact, they seem to be defining characters of modern culture, since I have drawn them from three of the most popular books of recent years: *Bridget Jones's Diary*, *High Fidelity* and *Prozac Nation*.

Today's generation desperately needs to hear that life is not hopeless; that it is possible to be loved; that we can be set free; that death is not the end.

But how will they hear this message? They do not come to our churches. They will not come to our events. They are not even on the fringes of the church. They are beyond the fringe. That is where most people are today.

So, if we are to reach them, we must go beyond the fringe. We must put out into the deep water. But if we are going to avoid drowning, it would be helpful to get some advice from people who are already out there, fishing effectively – because they are fishing biblically.

Therefore I have asked three good friends of mine to write about the approaches they have found particularly helpful as they have sought to go beyond the fringe.

Paul Harris is Head of Evangelism for the Evangelical Alliance UK. In his travels around the country he sees many churches which are effective in reaching their fringe but find it difficult to reach beyond. I first met Paul when he was vicar of a church in Southampton, where I live. At the time he was developing a marvellous way of reaching the community by visiting them and praying for them. Despite the ravages of secularism in our culture, there does seem to be a developing interest in spirituality in general and prayer in particular. It seems that a good way of reaching beyond the fringe is to begin by saying, 'Can I pray for you?' We have a gospel of spiritual power. Paul's approach seeks to include those who are currently excluded from that power.

Tony Watkins is a friend who also works for me in the Damaris Project. Through this project he is helping others to develop the same kind of knowledge and understanding of contemporary culture that he found vital through his years in student evangelism as a staff worker with UCCF. Many in today's culture do not want to hear us preach to them. But they are delighted to talk with us about the issues that interest them. Because the gospel is relevant to the whole of life, any subject that we discuss with people will provide a bridge for the gospel – as long as we understand the issues sufficiently and listen carefully enough to the culture. It seems that a good way of reaching beyond the fringe is to begin by saying to people, 'That's very interesting. Do tell me about it.' We have a gospel that makes the whole of life coherent. Tony's approach seeks to include those who are currently excluded from that coherence.

Phil Wall is a good friend who has been a great source of encouragement to me over the years, particularly when I have felt like giving up evangelism and doing something less difficult instead. Phil is currently Mission Team Leader with the Salvation Army. He has reached many people who are way beyond the fringe of the church through an approach that may seem strange, yet is exactly the approach that Jesus used on many occasions. Phil doesn't begin by giving people words, or indeed by giving them anything. Instead, he begins by asking them to help him. In so doing he makes himself vulnerable and makes them feel valuable. It seems that a good way of reaching beyond the fringe is to begin by saying, 'Can you help me, please?' We have a gospel that brings about a mutually dependent community. Phil's approach seeks to include those who are currently excluded from that community.

These ideas are not actually new. They go right back to biblical principles. They are not just techniques, because they have no value or power of their own. They each depend upon our having a genuine, prayerful love for those we are seeking to reach, and upon God's Holy Spirit to use them in order to bring people to himself.

But they are approaches which we must listen to and consider very carefully if we are serious about reaching people such as Bridget, Rob and Elizabeth.

Get up and go

NICK POLLARD

When the angel of the LORD appeared to Gideon,
he said, 'The LORD is with you, mighty warrior.'
'But sir,' Gideon replied, 'if the LORD is with us,
why has all this happened to us? Where are all
his wonders that our parents told us about when
they said, "Did not the LORD bring us up out of
Egypt?' But now the LORD has abandoned us and
put us into the hand of Midian.'
The LORD turned to him and said, 'Go in the
strength you have and save Israel out of Midian's
hand. Am I not sending you?' (Judg. 6:12–14).

It was many years ago that God told Gideon to stop
hiding away and to go out and do something that
would make a difference in the world. In the years
before and in those that followed, the Bible records many
other occasions when God told people to 'go'. This
regularly repeated command climaxes in Jesus' Great
Commission to the disciples in particular, and to all

Christians in general, to 'go into all the world'.

There is no doubt, then, that the God of the Bible is an outward-looking God who sends his people out into the world to make a difference. He is not an inward-looking God who wants to keep his people where they are, maintaining the *status quo*.

We know that we are meant to go – but how should we go? To think this through, it will be helpful to look more closely at God's call to Gideon. Although it was specific to Gideon, we can learn some general principles from it which we can usefully consider as we think about God's command to us.

First, if we are going to understand this part of the Bible, we have to see it in its proper context – as indeed we must do with any passage from the Bible. Otherwise we run the risk of being like the student who said that his favourite verse in the whole Bible was Isaiah 5:11, which says, 'Woe to those who rise early in the morning.' Isn't that a great verse for students? As long as it is taken out of context!

Some years before Gideon arrived on the scene, Moses had led the children of Israel out of Egypt and taken them through the desert. His successor, Joshua, subsequently led the people into the Promised Land, where they conquered the enemy through campaigns in the south and in the north.

Then Joshua died. In fact, all of those who came into the Promised Land with Joshua died. And a new generation grew up, a generation of people who didn't seem to know God or care about what he had done for them. Judges 2:10 describes it this way: 'After that whole generation had been gathered to their fathers, another generation grew up, who knew neither the LORD nor what he had done for Israel.'

An unknowing generation

This parallels the situation we face today. We, too, have a new generation of people who seem to know very little about God or what he has done for us. In our post-Christian culture an increasing number of people never go to a church or read the Bible. Nor do they even know what the Bible contains.

A few years ago my son was watching a Saturday morning TV quiz programme. It was one of those shows where children receive a prize if they answer a question correctly. But if they get it wrong, they are 'gunged' – a deluge of coloured goo is dropped all over them.

One contestant was a thirteen-year-old lad who was very clever. He answered every question correctly. He seemed to be the sort of child who could not only see the bottom line on an optician's chart but could also pronounce it – and translate it. My son became frustrated because he wanted to see this boy gunged. That appeared increasingly unlikely – until the questioner asked him, 'How many Gospels are there in the Bible?'

For the first time the boy looked puzzled. He did not have a clue. After a considerable pause, and looking far from confident, he ventured an answer. 'Twenty?'

Gunge!

Most of today's teenagers don't even believe that God exists. A recent survey of 18,000 school pupils aged between thirteen and fifteen found that only 39% of them believed in God. This state of ignorance will inevitably cause problems, because, believe it or not, we are designed to have God right in the centre of our lives and of our society. So living without him will have massive consequences for us as individuals and as a society, as it did for the people of Gideon's time.

The big crash

I have a newspaper cutting which tells of an event which happened a few years ago to a man called Kevin, who lives in Barry and drives a Cortina. In fact, what happens, I think, could only happen to a man called Kevin from Barry in a Cortina! The report is as follows:

> The trouble began when Kevin Jenkins and a friend tried to push start the Cortina on Tuesday night because the engine was damp. They pushed it on to a hill, but it gathered speed, and Mr Jenkins was unable to reach the brake. He chased it down the hill for two hundred yards as it careered into six parked cars and then watched as it crossed a junction, smashed through some railings and dropped a hundred feet on to the railway line in front of a passenger train. The Cortina was pushed along for half a mile before toppling on to another line – where it was hit by a coal train coming in the opposite direction. Yesterday all that remained of the car was the ignition key, its number plates and the cigar lighter. Police say they will be interviewing Mr Jenkins about possible traffic offences.

Kevin's car crashed because it didn't have a driver. Cars are designed to have a driver in the driving-seat, and if they run without one, disaster strikes. In the same way, we are designed to have God in the centre of our lives. If people or societies push God out, they, like that Cortina, will face disaster.

Occasionally such crashes in the lives of individuals and societies are obvious. We see individuals whose lives are devastated by alcohol or drug abuse, or the consequences of adultery. We see societies which are wrecked by crime or corruption. But, more often, the crashes are less visible. We don't necessarily see the pain and despair individuals experience in their hearts. Nor are we necessarily aware of the gradual disintegration of the society in which we live. (If you want to find out more about the hidden implications of a society which has rejected God, see my book *Why Do They Do That? Understanding Teenagers*, Lion, 1998.)

But whether we see them or not, these crashes are just as real as the one that happened to Kevin's Cortina. And they are just as inevitable if we push God out of the driving-seat of our lives and of our society.

We can see something like this demonstrated in the book of Judges. In fact, it happens twelve times in succession. The book describes twelve occasions in which, the writer says, 'again the Israelites did evil in the eyes of the LORD'. Each time, as they rejected God, their world crashed. Each time God then sent them a rescuer, called a judge. Thus God restored their lives and their society. But what did they then do? Once more they pushed God out of the driving-seat – and once more they crashed. In theological terms, this is a cycle of sin–judgment–grace–sin. And it occurred twelve times, with twelve different judges – one of whom was Gideon.

Before we meet Gideon, we are told that the children of Israel had become overrun by the Midianites, who spoiled their crops and killed their sheep, cattle and donkeys (Judg. 6:1–6). These problems had come because they had turned their backs on God. So what did they do? What do most people do when they face a disaster? They pray. Very few people are atheists when they are in trouble – or in an aircraft.

We will come back to this fact in Part 1 of this book. There we will consider how we can join with people in their desire to pray. We will see how we can reach beyond the fringe by praying for and with people.

A cry for help

But for now, let's look at how the children of Israel prayed. Notice that they didn't pray for forgiveness or to restore their relationship with God. The problems they were facing had come upon them because they had disobeyed God. But they didn't acknowledge that. Instead, they simply prayed for help. They were in dire need and they cried out to God.

Why should God have answered their prayer? They were facing problems because they had rebelled against God, but they hadn't really turned back to him or sought his forgiveness. So why should God have helped them? He would have been perfectly justified if he had refused to help. But he didn't. Instead, once more, he prepared to send them another rescuer. This time it was Gideon.

The angel of the LORD came to Gideon and said to him, 'The LORD is with you, mighty warrior.'

'But sir,' Gideon replied, 'if the LORD is with us, why has all this happened to us? ... the LORD has abandoned us and put us into the hand of Midian' (verses 12–13).

The angel and Gideon disagreed about the current state of affairs. The angel insisted that 'the LORD is with you'. But Gideon just couldn't believe that. He said, in effect, 'How can the LORD be with us?'

In fact, they were both correct. They were just talking about different things.

The angel was referring to Gideon as an individual when he said, 'the LORD is with you' (singular). But Gideon was referring to the children of Israel as he replied, 'How can the LORD be with us?' (plural). Both statements were correct.

It is true that, for a while, God had withdrawn from his people. This was not what God wanted, but it does seem to be the way that God reacts when people reject him. He doesn't immediately chase after them, but lets them go. If they have chosen to live without him, he doesn't overrule their decision. But he still loves those who reject him, and he wants to call them back. He seems to do this through individuals who still love him, as in the case of Gideon.

Although the Lord had withdrawn from Israel as a nation, he was still with Gideon as an individual. It seems that Gideon was a godly man who wanted to follow the Lord even though his nation did not. And God now set out to use him to call others back to himself.

Once more we can see a parallel with our society today. There is no doubt that our culture has turned its back upon God (again, see *Why Do They Do That?* for a detailed description of the development of that rejection through the eighteenth, nineteenth and twentieth centuries). Consequently, there is a real sense in which God has withdrawn from our country. If we, as a culture, have chosen to live without God, he is not going to overrule us and impose himself upon us. But we are going to face the consequences that stem from pushing him out of the driving-seat.

While God does seem to have withdrawn from our nation, however, he is still with individuals. No matter how much our society has turned its back on God, he does still have his individuals who love him and want to follow him. As with Gideon, God wants to use them to make a difference and to change the world.

That is why it is important for Christians to hear God's

call to go out and serve him in the world, rather than just staying in church among the other individuals who already love God.

Someone has said that Christians are like manure.. If manure is spread across a field it does a lot of good. But if it is heaped together in one place, it stinks. Unfortunately, a lot of churches stink. They are simply places where groups of Christians huddle together trying to protect themselves from the ravages of the world around, instead of going out to be salt and light in a godless culture.

When we look at the tragic 'crashes' happening in the world around us, we are tempted to ask, 'What's wrong with the world?' That is not really the right question. We know what is wrong with the world: it has rejected God and is facing the dreadful consequences. The question we need to ask is, 'What is wrong with Christians?' Why is it that we are not being salt and light in the world? Why is it that we are not making a difference?

What is wrong with Christians?

Part of the answer to this question is that we struggle to understand the world around us. If we are to make a difference in this world, we need to understand it. Gideon did. He knew about the world in which he lived. He knew about the history and heritage of his culture (verse 13). He knew about the enemy which had infiltrated it. He knew where to find the Midianite camp, and how to attack it (7:1, 17–18). Like the men of Issachar, he 'understood the times and knew what Israel should do' (1 Chr. 12:32).

We also must understand the times. That is not a new concept. Missionaries have known this for years. Before they are sent on to the mission field they are taught about the culture in which they will be working. Similarly, those of us who are seeking to make a difference in today's world must try to understand the roots of the ideas, beliefs and values that are shaping it. We need missionary training to stay at home. We will look at this in Part 2 as we consider how some understanding of the people, books, films, magazines and music that are shaping contemporary culture can help us to reach those beyond the fringe.

But no matter how much training and preparation we have, it will be of no value to us at all unless we also obey God's command to 'go'. Gideon heard that call clearly and obeyed it, and so should we in our own circumstances.

Gideon was told explicitly by the Lord to 'Go in the strength you have and save Israel out of Midian's hand' (6:14). This is a straightforward command. It was specific to Gideon. But it is part of a general call which is given to us all throughout the Bible.

I love the Bible in all its complexity and depth. We will never mine all the treasures that it contains this side of heaven. The more we look at it, the more we find in it. But at the same time, the Bible is also profoundly simple. It essentially contains two commands. There is the command to *come* and the command to *go*.

The Bible tells us that we must come to Jesus. It commands people everywhere to repent. We must come to him, acknowledge that we have done wrong, ask him to forgive us, invite him to fill us with his Spirit, and receive the new life that he has for us.

These are commands; they are not options. The Bible doesn't say, 'If you've got nothing else to do on a wet Sunday afternoon, you might like to come and receive a bit of forgiveness.' These are imperatives. We are commanded to come.

The call to every Christian

Once we have come to Jesus, we are commanded to go. This, too, is not an option. It's not just for a few special people. It's for all of us. Every Christian is called to go out and share God's love in a hurting world.

We might think that that is not our job. Going out into the world sounds so difficult and frightening. Perhaps we might do other things instead – like some of the practical jobs in the church. Of course, it is important that these practical jobs are done. But the Bible tells us that these are in addition to going out and sharing God's love, not instead of it.

That is made very clear in chapters 6 – 8 in the book of Acts. At the beginning of chapter 6, the twelve apostles decided that they should appoint seven men to do the administrative work. They were to do all the practical jobs in the church. The text records their names: Stephen, Philip, Procorus, Nicanor, Timon, Parmenas and Nicolas.

The next few pages follow events in the lives of two of these characters, Stephen and Philip. And they clearly show that these men, who had been specifically set aside to do in-house practical tasks, were also engaged in frontline evangelism.

Stephen preached to the Sanhedrin. As a consequence he was stoned to death (Acts 7). Then Philip travelled to Samaria, where he preached to the crowds, cast out demons and healed the sick. He was later taken to the Ethiopian eunuch, spoke to him personally and led him to faith in Christ (Acts 8).

There we see a wide range of evangelism carried out by two people who were set aside to do administrative tasks. So there is no way we can say that we are called to serve only in practical, internal ways. Whatever else we are called to do, we are all called to go out into the world.

Of course, the fact that we are all given this command doesn't make it any easier to obey. It's much easier to stay in church; indeed, it's much safer there.

I recently read some accident statistics. (I have a rich and varied reading life!) It seems that 20% of accidents happen in the car, 17% at home, 16% in the air, on the railways or at sea, and 0.0001% in church.

So there you are! If you want a comfortable, easy life, stay in church, because it's far safer there. Of course it is. If only it wasn't! Then none of us would want to hide away there.

Phil Wall, in his excellent book *I'll Fight*, recounts an event which happened in the old Soviet Union. A group of Christians were meeting in a church to pray, when a number of KGB soldiers rushed in with Kalashnikov rifles. 'We are going to shoot all the Christians in this room,' they shouted. 'If you are not a Christian, leave now.'

Some people left, but others stayed.

The soldiers said to those who remained, 'You don't seem to understand. We are going to shoot all the Christians who are here. If you are not really a Christian, this is your last opportunity to leave. Go now.'

A few more left, but some stayed.

The KGB men then looked at the few who were left. 'So you are Christians, and you are prepared to die for your faith?'

'Yes, we are,' they replied.

'Well, that won't be necessary,' said the soldiers as they put down their guns, 'because we want to become Christians too. We just needed to know that you were genuine.'

If you had been in that room, would you have stayed or gone? Are you so passionate about following Jesus that you will go wherever he sends you and do whatever he says, or are you just after a cosy, comfy life? Martin Luther King said, 'A belief not worth dying for is not worth living for.'

We don't face Kalashnikov rifles, but we do face ridicule and rejection. Sadly, that rejection sometimes comes from other Christians who can't understand why we want to be out in the world instead of huddled in the church with them.

I know a young woman who took the command of Christ seriously when she went to university. She didn't want to stay closeted among Christians, but wanted rather to be salt and light in the wider student world. So, as well as joining the Christian Union, she joined the feminist group. Consequently, she faced criticism from other Christian students. They couldn't understand why she wanted to be a part of this group. They thought she was putting herself in danger.

Of course, she was. It wasn't safe and easy. But we're at war, and who has ever heard of a safe war? Through her involvement in the feminist group, she was able to reach many individuals who would never have gone to a Christian Union meeting, much less to church. But through her they were able to understand something of the Christian message of God's love for all people.

Moreover, she was able not only to help individuals, but also to exercise a fair and reasonable influence on the policy of the Feminist Society. One day, the group passed a resolution to give money to a student who wanted to have an abortion but couldn't afford it. My friend was able to encourage them to consider whether this was a just decision. At her suggestion, they added another resolution – that they would give equal amounts of money to students who could not afford to keep their babies but did not want an abortion.

God with us, us with the people

Thus my friend was able to make a difference not just to individuals but also to the wider society around. That is what incarnational evangelism is all about. Indeed, that is what any kind of evangelism is all about. Incarnational evangelism is not a special type of evangelism. All evangelism is incarnational. We are called to be there with people, working with them.

These 'people' are not some strange group who live miles away from us. They may be beyond the fringe, but many of them are also on our doorstep. Indeed, when Jesus told his disciples to go, he told them to start in their own backyard. He said that they were to be witnesses 'in Jerusalem, Judea, Samaria and the ends of the earth'. That is, they were to start where they were, and move out into the wider locality before tackling the whole world.

If that is the pattern that we should follow, perhaps we also should start with those around us. There are plenty there to work with.

It never ceases to amaze me when Christians tell me that they don't have any non-Christian friends. Since there are far more non-Christians than Christians in our country, we have to work pretty hard to have friends who are exclusively drawn from the small Christian community. To achieve that amazing feat, we have to live in a way that cuts us off from non-Christians. That is possible only if we contort our diaries so much that we spend most of our time at church, or in church meetings.

If we come out of church, however, and just get on with life in the world around, we will find that we have many non-Christian friends. We don't have to go far. We will find many non-Christians in our street, outside our children's school gates or at work. They are there. All we need to do is to make the most of the opportunities.

I am fortunate to live in a house which is ideal for parties. It has big rooms and a great garden. So we hold a lot of celebrations, from Christmas to Bonfire Night. When we have a party we don't just invite people from church. That would be a bit strange, given that many of them live quite a long way away. Rather, we invite all our neighbours. Most of them are not Christians. But most of them have now become our friends.

If we look out from our church-preoccupied lives, we will find that there are many people who would be delighted to be our friends. Not all of us find it easy to make friends. But we find it less difficult if we follow the example of Jesus. He made friends with many people, even unlikely ones. But he often struck up those friendships not just by talking to them, or by doing something for them, but by asking *them* to do something for *him*. He asked them if they could help him by providing a meal, or somewhere to stay, or a drink of water.

We will think more about this in Part 3, when we consider how we might reach beyond the fringe by asking people to help us. And when we have done that, we will come back again to Gideon.

PART 1

Praying with the world

PAUL HARRIS

Introduction

NICK POLLARD

'I cannot believe that God exists,' John said forcefully as he put down his empty beer glass. We had been talking together for a while in the Students Union bar, and now the conversation had wound its way around to spiritual issues.

'Can I get you another drink?' I asked. He couldn't refuse that offer, and so we settled down to talk for a long time about the evidence for the existence of God.

As the conversation progressed, we didn't seem to get very far philosophically but we made a lot of progress in our relationship. A warm friendship developed between us. We could talk together comfortably about personal issues as well as philosophical ones. It wasn't long before the conversation drifted naturally in that direction.

John began to talk about the problems he was facing. His mum and dad had recently divorced and he wasn't at all sure which of them he was going to stay with in the next vacation. He wasn't even sure he wanted to continue at university at all. His course was not what he had expected, and he didn't get on terribly well with the others in his hall.

Tears began to form in his eyes as he spoke about the turmoil and pain he was experiencing. After we had talked for some while, I asked gently, 'Would you like me to pray for you?'

He thought for a moment and then said, 'Yes, please.'

That may sound bizarre. Here was a student who, not long before, had argued adamantly that God does not exist. And now he wanted me to pray.

This is by no means unusual. There are many people like John. In fact, almost all the non-Christians I meet day by day are keen to be prayed for.

The spiritual as a bridge

There is a paradox in the culture around us. People may argue that there is no God. They may live as if God does not exist. And yet there is a widespread interest in spirituality in general, and in prayer in particular.

That shouldn't really surprise us. We know that every individual has an inbuilt desire to know God. Anthropologists tell us that wherever we might go in the world, we will find people who are in some way religious, seeking some form of spiritual fulfilment.

Since the eighteenth century, this has been overlaid in western culture by a rejection of the supernatural and an emphasis on the scientific method. We have been persuaded that spirituality is to be rejected in favour of (so-called) independent reason and (so-called) objective facts.

For most people, however, this viewpoint has only partly won. Despite the influence of secular humanism and scientific materialism, most people still sense that there is something beyond the physical world. They desire some form of spiritual experience and are open to explore ways in which they might achieve it.

A lot of people have a split view of reality. They hold two contradictory assumptions. They accept the spiritual realm and are eager to explore it. Yet they also reject the spiritual realm as incompatible with reason and evidence. Despite the clash between these assumptions, they can be held in tension because they work at different levels. The first is expressed at the level of experience, or what is sometimes called 'personal truth'. The second is expressed at the level of argument, or what is sometimes called 'propositional truth'.

If our evangelism consists solely of propositions which we present and defend, we may find that we bump into a wall of rejection, built on the asumption that a belief in the spiritual realm is incompatible with reason and evidence. But, if our evangelism offers people opportunities to express their desire for spiritual experience, we may find that we encounter a bridge built on their willingness to explore and experience the spiritual realm.

That doesn't mean that we should abandon propositions or reasoned argument in favour of spiritual experience alone. In Part 2 we will consider how we might reach beyond the fringe by talking with people in the form of propositions and reasoned argument. For some people and at some times, however, that may not be the best starting-point.

Ultimately, we want to help people to discover that the gospel is a whole message for the whole person. Therefore, in time, we will want to help people to discover that true evidence and reason are, in fact, compatible with true spiritual experience.

But such an integrated perspective may be approached

from many angles. The key to helping people to consider rational, propositional truth may be to start with personal spiritual experience.

Paul Harris calls us to begin by offering to pray for people. This approach opened doors into John's heart and mind. Once he had agreed that I could pray for him, he not only became more open to exploring the realm of spiritual experience; he also became much more open and receptive to the rational arguments about the existence of God that he had previously rejected out of hand.

Praying with the world

PAUL HARRIS

1. Prayer beyond the fringe

An Eskimo was crouched inscribing a neat circle on the ice, his fishing-rod at his side, when he thought he heard a voice: 'There are no fish under the ice!'

Looking around and seeing no-one, he dismissed the thought and began to cut the circle he had marked out.

The voice, louder and more urgent, boomed out: 'There are *no* fish under the ice!'

The Eskimo looked up and said, 'Is that you, God?'

'No,' came the reply. 'It's the manager of the ice rink!'

All too often, the church makes the same mistake. Poised and ready for action, desperate to be effective 'fishers of people', its members find themselves fishing in the wrong place. They are frustrated when what they took to be a good evangelistic opportunity proves fruitless. The reason: they have not understood the setting, a failing that has arisen because they have lost touch with their roots in the local community.

'The Word became flesh and blood and moved into the neighbourhood' (John 1:14, *The Message*). To be effective, the form and style of Christian ministry and mission should express the message of the gospel before a word is uttered. This is not a question of smart communication – 'the medium is the message' – but rather a reflection of the way God himself operates. There is no message, mission or ministry without people and place. Mission must be 'fleshed out'. Jesus 'moved into the neighbourhood'.

When the church expresses evangelism primarily as theory and technique, as programmes and projects, it is losing the plot. Research, planning and training all have their place, providing that Christians have first recognized that it is what they *are* rather than what they *do* that impresses those they are trying to reach. Unless this happens, there will be little fruit, and the training that is offered, far from helping Christians to feel equipped and encouraged, will instead compound their sense of inadequacy. So they go round the loop again: guilt – action – failure – inactivity – convinced that evangelism is bad news rather than good, and is best left to the specially gifted experts.

Some years ago, a leading evangelical churchman had a young colleague who was fervent in praying for the people of their area but reluctant to visit them. The older man encouraged his assistant with the following blunt advice: 'Young man, your prayers need legs!'

I do not know whether this had the desired effect on the curate in question, but the words have echoed in my mind since my first boss in Christian ministry 'encouraged' me with them. Prayer seldom comes easily, and door-to-door visiting is the ultimate torture for many. Yet one of the most exciting aspects of ministry I have known has involved a combination of these two activities.

There is much talk these days of the importance of prayer underpinning any evangelistic enterprise. There has been an apparent increase in prayer networks and initiatives at national, regional and local levels. In some quarters 'prayer-walking' has become popular as areas are staked out and 'claimed' by Christians who walk round them Joshua-style, either silently or with much trumpeting and banging of drums. I am sure that God in his wisdom and sovereign way uses a host of approaches, and I have no desire to denigrate any of the above endeavours. On the contrary, I have initiated prayer walks myself (the quieter version). Despite this, I am left with the feeling that prayer and evangelism remain separated in theory and in practice. Like a couple in the TV programme *Blind Date*, prayer and evangelism wriggle off their stools and step forward as God's chosen pairing only for the dividing screen to stay in place rather than slipping back so that they can embrace.

In the local church, one group prays while another visits. At a large evangelistic event, some will pray in a back room while the more extrovert speakers and musicians minister out front. This is certainly a good thing in those settings, but it reinforces the notion that prayer and evangelism are separate endeavours, with the former there primarily to serve the latter. My aim in this section is to highlight a context in which prayer and evangelism meet. This is not a 'Just add water for results' manual which reduces prayer to a technique and evangelism to a human effort which God is obliged to bless. Rather, I hope to share some of the lessons one church learned when they combined prayer and door-to-door visiting as part of their outreach to the community they wished to serve. You will find some practical tips and some mistakes to avoid, and smile at some of the funny incidents which happened along the way.

More important than the practicalities, however, are the

principles and assumptions we followed or stumbled upon as we set about visiting and praying. I address the question of whether this idea could work in other settings. I believe that the experience of others shows that it could, provided that the guiding principles have been taken on board.

I also include the stories of some of those who were affected by this programme of prayer and visiting. This may provide an element of human interest, but also reinforces the crucial point that God follows his own time-scale in his dealings with individuals as much as when dealing with the universe at large. Although this should be obvious, my experience suggests that we often impose our own time-frame, with disastrous consequences for the hapless individuals caught up in our evangelistic efforts. In fishing terms, we need to develop patience rather than striking too early at the first sign of a bite. In what follows, the names of some people have been changed as appropriate.

2. First footings

'I've seen vicars come and go. They all try to change things, but the church goes on regardless.' My wife Cathy heard these blunt words shortly after our arrival in the parish of Bitterne, Southampton. The statement was not calculated to discourage; indeed, the man who uttered them was, as I would discover, deeply spiritual with a great heart for prayer.

When searching for a new vicar, the church had stated that they wanted to grow in prayer, engage more with the community and develop a pattern of worship which was more accessible to those outside the church. These were to be priorities, and, like most other churches, they also wanted their new pastor to exhibit a range of qualities which might make even the archangel Gabriel think twice about applying for the post. It is probably just as well that spiritual realists such as the man mentioned exist as a foil to the sometimes unrealistic expectations of clergy and selection panels.

The context

Bitterne is a clearly identifiable community to the east of Southampton. Once a village overlooking the old port, then a leafy suburb, it is now best described as a 'middle ring' community lying between the centre and the city limits. It is made up of largely 1930s owner-occupied housing with estates of low-rise council flats built in the 1960s. For an urban community, it is remarkably settled, many of the people working in the docks, on the ships or at the reduced yet still prosperous Vosper-Thorneycroft shipbuilding yard. The community is conservative in many of its values and views. On the political front, however, it is a different story. All three local councillors belonged to the Labour Party, as does the sitting MP. It might be described as a lower-middle- or upper-working-class area, although these terms never tell the whole story.

The parish church stands at the heart of the community, with its towering spire and leafy approach a reminder of bygone rural days. Local residents, even the younger ones, talk about popping down to the village centre – a term which, given the supermarkets, subways and sliproads around the central pedestrian precinct, seems inappropriate to the newcomer. Bitterne has a flourishing local history society and a small heritage centre which contribute to the continuing sense of community.

Despite the local seafaring tradition, we found that not many young people fixed their sights on distant horizons. Some went away to college, and there were a few who had moved into the area, but they were the exception rather than the norm. Young couples set up home in or near the area, content to stay close to supportive parents and grandparents. Through the church schools and youth programme we would often meet youngsters whose parents and even grandparents we were meeting in other pastoral contexts. There was a flourishing 'village' grapevine, hungry for rumours and gossip. I sensed that this network could work in the church's favour. Positive reaction to developments in church life were passed on just as quickly and with as much exaggeration as negative.

Years ago at theological college, I asked a fellow student in his final year what sort of place he hoped to begin his ordained ministry in. He replied that he and his wife wanted to serve in a community which they could put their arms around and love in God's name. His answer has stuck with me. Despite being a city parish, Bitterne was just that. It had a sense of its own identity, and was not too large – about 11,000 people in just under 4,000 homes.

In the late 1960s and 1970s a dual-carriage expressway into the city had been carved through the heart of the 'village'. The accompanying redevelopment swept away the recreation ground, the village church schools and a number of the older houses. Despite some new facilities, the locals were left with the feeling of having been assaulted or abused. Over a quarter of a century later the feeling of grievance was still strong in the communal memory.

This sense of a hurt done to the community is by no means isolated. Memories are long, and any who hope to reach a community with the gospel must first become acquainted with local history.

The sense of pain in the community of Bitterne was compounded by the fact that the late 1960s had been a difficult period in the life of the parish church. Long-standing members would seldom talk about it openly, but, with knowing looks to one another, would refer to 'that dark chapter'. (The details of whatever dispute there had been were shrouded in mystery.) One woman said to me early on, 'You won't divide the church, will you?' The memories were strong nearly twenty years after the event. As I visited in the area, I would meet people who were evidently part of the fallout from that time.

I knew from my short time as a police officer the value of being seen out and about in the community. Cycling round the parish, walking the kids to school, and chatting in the playground, shops and precinct all helped to raise the profile. Ordinary people responded warmly to a friendly, personal approach. Hitherto a reluctant dog-collar wearer, I even wore the white plastic 'ring of confidence' more than in any previous parish. The apostle Paul's words about becoming all things to all people so that by all possible means he might see some saved (1 Cor. 9:22) were a consolation in this respect.

The concept

Can a church ever be content with the quality of its prayer life? Probably not – any more than individuals ever are. Prayer cannot be quantified, although prayerlessness is quickly apparent. Like many large evangelical Anglican churches, Bitterne Church (whose most recent membership list showed over 500 adults) had a long-standing commitment to prayer for overseas mission partners, with regular mission news slots in the services. There had been a prayer triplet scheme, although sadly this had faded by the time of our arrival in the summer of 1993. A monthly prayer card was produced; there was a list of prayer requests for those who were sick or bereaved, and a faithful healing prayer group met regularly. On special occasions there would be a reasonable turnout for evenings and half-nights of prayer.

Sadly, this was not matched by a commitment to regular gatherings for prayer, although I was aware that some church members were very committed and faithful in praying for the life and mission of the church. It is a mistake to judge the quality of a church's prayer life by the number attending a designated prayer meeting. As a church fellowship, however, we needed a deeper prayer life and an increase in the scope and regularity of our praying.

My two immediate predecessors, the late Michael Perry (the gifted hymnwriter and liturgist) and Jeff Watson (now Archdeacon of Ely) had understood the importance of knowing the area they were working in. Since both of them were more methodical and better organized than I, the church office was equipped with lists of the streets and blocks of flats and a card index listing church members and pastoral contacts street by street.

There was also a well-established network of area pastors. These were senior church members who shared in the pastoral care of church members and in following up baptism, wedding and funeral contacts. Each of these committed people had a network of helpers who delivered tracts and invitations to harvest, Christmas and Easter services. This system had much to commend it, and it probably compares favourably with the community structures of similar churches. I could not help feeling, however, that it was limited in terms of meaningful engagement with the majority of people living in our area.

My colleague at the time, David Snuggs, and I had regular days away for prayer and long-term planning. On one of these, we spent some time pondering what might help to stimulate the church's prayer for the community while encouraging individuals to be more systematic in their personal prayers. Having drawn up a plan, we did not come away with a sense of having made an earth-shattering discovery. In fact, we felt rather sheepish: what we had decided seemed a bit 'churchy'. We liked to think that we were part of the new breed of radical clergy, full of creative, image-busting, ground-breaking ideas. We were open to new expressions of church life and were already involved in plans to plant a new church. Despite our coloured clerical shirts and best intentions, however, we proposed to hold a twice-weekly 9am prayer service in the parish church, at which we would pray through the streets of the parish in alphabetical order, one on each day. It was hardly headline-grabbing stuff!

Just an innocent question

Among the many suggestions and schemes we had put forward, this was one of the few that was not met by a chorus of disapproval from one quarter of the church or another. It was unthreatening, and in any case it is a mark of 'spiritual correctness' never to oppose suggestions for more prayer. Even if one has no intention of actually joining in the latest prayer initiative oneself, it is comforting to know that one belongs to a church which takes prayer seriously.

The first Tuesday morning saw about eight members present in the front pews of the side chapel. We used a short set order of service, called Shorter Morning Prayer. This was hardly a revivalist prayer meeting! At the end there was a time of open prayer, during which I mentioned a couple of requests from the first road on the list. This happened to be the cul-de-sac in which the curate's house was situated. These requests were based on some notes from David, who, typically, was in touch with the needs of his neighbours. Those present shared enthusiastically in the prayer time.

As we were getting up to go, one of the group, a younger area pastor with a real heart for prayer, asked me, 'Which street are we praying for on Thursday?'

After a moment's thought, I gave her the name of another street beginning with the letter A. I felt slightly ashamed to realize that I was thinking in a piecemeal fashion while she was wanting to think ahead and to prepare herself for prayer. This is one of the hallmarks of a real intercessor that I have come to recognize, and now look out for when I visit a new city or area in my current work.

On my way back to the vicarage, I passed between the graves of two of my predecessors as vicars of Bitterne (always a sobering thing to do!) when the Holy Spirit came upon me and I heard a voice saying, 'Paul, go and visit the road you have just mentioned.'

I am not really a 'hotline to God man'; the preceding sentence is my Acts-style recording of what happened. Actually, I *was* between the aforesaid graves when the thought struck me, 'If Sandra wants to know in advance who we're praying for, why don't we let the people themselves know we're going to pray for them? Could be interesting, and it probably won't do any harm!'

Hotline or not, I suspected that this was God at work. Typically of him, however, he left me plenty of space to choose. I could dismiss this as an idle thought, or I could believe it was a divine nudge which I had the freedom to ignore or to obey. I have plenty to learn about discerning the voice of God, and I wish I was more obedient. On that occasion I went home, did a token amount of admin and headed off on foot for somewhere beginning with A.

An hour later, I knocked on my first door. No reply. Next door the same. Had I mis-heard? The fourth door I recognized; I had been here before. It opened to reveal a man in his early seventies. He seemed pleased to see me. I remembered his name; I had taken his wife's funeral some months previously and had visited once since then. I explained that we would be praying for him and his neighbours in a couple of days' time, and asked whether there was anything he would like us to pray for specifically for him. He was evidently moved by this – a reaction I was to see many times in the ensuing months and years. He asked simply for God's strength and unselfishly mentioned a neighbour two doors down who had gone into hospital that week for an operation. I made a note of her name and her house number on the back of the envelope I had brought with me (organized as ever), wished him well and headed on.

Three houses further on I got another answer. The door was opened by a girl I recognized from the top year of the church junior school. I was one of the governors and went in regularly to do assemblies or to share in lessons. She looked embarrassed, and I asked if her mother was in. The girl retreated, and her mother Anne, a normally cheery woman with whom I usually exchanged greetings in the school playground, came down the hall. I explained why I was calling. As soon as I mentioned the word 'prayer', she said, 'You can pray for us. Janey's been missing all night. She's literally just come home.'

I stepped into the hall and the story tumbled out. I chatted with Janey and her mum together, made some suggestions about practical help and promised to pray for them. Anne was amazed that I had called at just that point; in her words, 'It's like God sent you.' Little did she know! (Some time later I took a service of blessing for Anne and her new husband, and had a fruitful link with the family through the rest of my time in the area.)

Less than two hours later I 'returned home with joy'

like the disciples (Luke 10:17). I had not cast out demons or stormed the gates of hell, but I had seen God open doors. This crazy, quaint scheme could work. There's a saying which appealed to me the first time I heard it: 'If you want to serve God, see where he's at work and join in!' I was reminded that morning that God is already working beyond the fringe, and that's where I needed to join in. I was not taking him there; he had gone ahead, as he always does.

The next day I told David what had happened and suggested that we start to visit two roads a week. By my reckoning it would take about fourteen months to get round them all. He was enthusiastic, and that is how we began.

It is easy to exaggerate the amount of thought that goes into evangelistic projects like this, and the extent of their success. We are called to be 'fishers of men' (and women), but this does not give us licence to tell fishermen's tales. Too often I have heard church leaders trying to top each other's stories of encouragement. ('We had an unchurched person *this* big!') The insecurity which such behaviour reflects is why so many church leaders finish up frustrated as 'keepers of aquaria' instead of being 'fishers of men' – but that is another story! If God turns up big time, he does not need us to stage-manage his special effects for him.

This initiative was not part of a patiently worked-out strategy for reaching our community, but simply a result of a passion to reach a whole community for God and an awareness of our inadequacy in prayer. In the light of what happened in the following years, I would make it the centrepiece of any future strategy to reach beyond the fringe of the church with God's love.

The widow's tale

One of my favourite apocryphal clergy stories is the one about the young curate who went out visiting in the parish. At the first door he called at, he was greeted by a little old lady who flung her arms out towards him, exclaiming, 'Cliff Richard!' Parrying her intended embrace, he accepted the customary cup of tea.

Surprised but undaunted, he went on to his next call, only for the same thing to happen. Having escaped being clutched to a matronly bosom, and pondering deeply on the popularity of 'St Cliff', he tried one more house. Here a shapely young blonde opened the door, shrieking, 'Cliff Richard!' as she beckoned him in. At that point the curate broke into song: 'Got myself a cryin', walkin', sleepin', talkin', livin' doll!'

On my visits, I have never been mistaken for the singing knight; the gas man or the double-glazing salesman, maybe. There have been times, however, when people have seen me as an angel, strange though that may sound.

One such occasion was the afternoon I called on the door of a neat little bungalow in a quiet cul-de-sac. The door opened, and there stood a short, elderly lady, a brown envelope in her hand and tears running down her face. Before I could speak, she said, 'Oh, God must have sent you, you're like an angel!'

I recognized her as Vera, someone who had been bereaved earlier in the year; David had taken her husband's funeral. I went in, and she crumpled as she explained how she had just opened a letter from the hospital, calling her late husband for an appointment. She felt that this had set her back months in the process of grieving. I did my best to comfort her by listening as she talked about her husband, showing me some pictures of him. I reassured her of our support and offered to pray for her there and then – an offer which she gratefully accepted.

Vera could not get over the fact that I had called at just the right moment, even though I had thought I was simply making a routine call. There were about 4,000 other doors I could have called on that afternoon, but God had sent me there! From the start of our visiting we found that this sort of thing was a regular occurrence. I saw this as a mark of God's sovereign grace and also a measure of the needs among our community.

After the visit I mentioned to a caring Christian neighbour that Vera had been upset, explained why, and asked her to make contact soon. Over the coming months, there were other difficult days for Vera as she continued to travel through her bereavement. She started coming to the midweek communion service at the parish church – a peaceful service which many who felt emotionally bruised and raw seemed to value as a quiet way into worship. She accepted an invitation to one of the bereavement courses.

In time, she came on an Alpha course, and now looks back on that as the time when she came to know God's love in a deep and personal way. Since then she has become a regular in the Alpha team. Her cheery manner, which had served her well in her years as a conductress on the city buses, is much appreciated and shines through the clouds of grief which still blow along from time to time.

3. Motives and methods, do's and don'ts

The common people heard him gladly (Mark 12:37, AV).

After only a few weeks we had the feeling of having struck gold. Christians in Britain get so used to hearing about declining church numbers and to seeing the results of godlessness in society that it is all too easy to allow a siege mentality to creep over us. If we are ever to reach effectively beyond the fringe, we have to face and then overcome this expectation of rejection. If not, we will be defensive and fearful, and our expectation will become a self-fulfilling prophecy. There is a balance to be struck. We cannot assume that people will be desperate to hear us or to receive us; we have to work for a hearing and make an effort to communicate. At the same time, we need to cultivate and to pray for a godly winsomeness, a confidence that never comes across as smugness. Confidence breeds confidence.

Without being complacent, we quickly realized that

48

people were genuinely pleased to see us. I wished I had a pound for every person who said something like, 'You're the first vicar just to call for no special reason.' (Of course, I would have given a percentage of the money to Tearfund!) Even people who declared that they were not religious, as many did, felt that it was good to see the church getting involved in this way. Many people asked us to pray, some invited us in to pray then and there, and word got round the village grapevine that the church was doing something good. From time to time we even had people who did not normally attend church turn up on the morning when we were praying for their road. This was a bonus!

In the course of the first fourteen months – our first circuit, as it were – I could count on the fingers of one hand the number of times people were rude or abusive. None of those occasions came close to crucifixion! Why were people so receptive?

Why people listened

The prophets of doom have got it wrong

While the harmful effects of nominal belief must not be underestimated, there has not been a wholesale move away from spiritual things. There is, if anything, a greater spiritual awareness today, but this is not matched by a spiritual alertness. In 1997 the Christian Research Association reported in *Religious Trends* that 71% of people said they believed in God, and that two in three (65%) called themselves Christians. Two years previously, the British Social Attitudes Survey revealed that 56% of those asked claimed some degree of belief in God. There is no room for complacency here, but such figures should temper our pessimism as we engage with those outside the church. There is something with which we may connect if we approach people in the right way.

The outpouring of grief over the death of Diana, Princess of Wales, in August 1997 was interpreted by some as a sign of a new spiritual and emotional awakening. My own view is rather that it represented in some way a religious echo in the communal memory of society. People may not go to church in great numbers, but they have not become entirely irreligious. At the time of Diana's death, which seemed to trigger expressions of previously suppressed grief in many, people instinctively felt the need to make some gesture. In Bitterne, wreaths, tributes, poems and pictures were spread out spontaneously in two places: outside the church and outside the main supermarket.

As we visited around Bitterne, we saw plenty of evidence of latent or residual spirituality. Since prayer was on the agenda, many people claimed to pray regularly. Allowing for those who were making the right noises to get the 'spiritual truancy' officers off their doorstep, it seemed to us that many, especially the older generation, were still 'saying their prayers'.

People still value community

It is generally accepted that we live in a fragmented society as part of an accelerating culture. The word 'community' is used frequently to describe groupings of people who are loosely connected and who rarely meet in person. We speak about the 'gay community', and on the internet categories of information are presented as communities. Meanwhile, back at pavement level on planet Earth, many people feel dislocated or isolated in their local environment. Even the stronger community identity in Bitterne was fuelled largely by looking back to a shared hurt – the building of the bypass. In other urban and rural settings I have discovered a valuing of community even though this sometimes draws strength from a sense of being under siege: the estate mentality, the threat of land development, and so on.

In Bitterne, we stressed that we were going to pray for people and their neighbours. In other words, we were recognizing small units within the community, and assuming neighbourhood links which may or may not have been present. People seemed to respond positively to this. The fact that we were aware of the possibility of shared needs in the community and that we were doing something about them (however strange the idea of praying about speeding cars on an estate might be!) reinforced people's notion of community.

Our prayers had legs

From time to time people would express the view that it would be better for us to be doing something positive rather than 'just praying'. Fair comment. This was not a cue for us sanctimoniously to harp on about the importance of prayer. At times like this we would agree that action was important, and gently mention some of the features of our involvement with the community: the lunch clubs, playgroups, community care scheme, parenting course, bereavement course, the open youth club and the fact that the church's private tennis courts had been converted into a floodlit basketball and five-a-side football area for the community. We did this not to correct them but to connect with their expressed concern.

We should not consider praying for any community

unless we are prepared to get involved with the needs of that community. Such involvement may well be costly, will not be widely appreciated, and may leave us feeling used. But our prayers do need legs. Sometimes, as we visited, we could not help becoming aware of individual needs. The hard-working area pastors could not be expected to pick these up. We soon realized that we would have to develop pastoral teams in each of the eight areas of the parish. Working under the existing area pastors, these teams were an additional spin-off from the prayer initiative and a further expression of our commitment to teams throughout the life of the church.

Not evangelism in disguise

When people ask me what I do, I brace myself for their response when I tell them. My job title is Head of the Evangelism Department for the Evangelical Alliance UK. As soon as they hear the word 'evangelism' reinforced by 'evangelical', they wince or their eyes glaze over. Small-talk about the weather or the fortunes of Chelsea Football Club may follow.

One reason evangelism has fallen into disrepute is that forms of evangelism have often lacked integrity. The activities I have in mind are those which purport to be one thing but which actually turn out to be something else. For instance, I have seen Christians using questionnaires in shopping centres. These start out as apparently innocuous market research, but clumsily change gear two-thirds of the way through, asking a question such as, 'And have you ever wondered what will happen to you when you die?' All of us have experienced the telesales approach, where callers spend five minutes telling us that this is not a sales call but a piece of genuine independent research. We despise them: do they think we are stupid? When they finally ask whether we have considered installing double-glazing or stone cladding, I, for one, would happily go to their office there and then and install something large in their noses!

Evangelistic projects which lack integrity may well provide the Christians involved with gung-ho stories to tell around the camp-fire when they return to the safety of the Christian enclave. But they often leave their victims feeling deceived and used. This is contrary to the gospel, and so, the sovereignty of God notwithstanding, we should not be surprised that such endeavours produce little, if any, lasting fruit.

Our prayer visiting was not evangelism in disguise. We stated precisely and succinctly what we were doing. We were calling to say hello and to see if there was anything they wanted us to pray for when we prayed for their street in a couple of days' time. It was not a way of angling for that old evangelical trophy 'the good conversation'. We were not begging for money, asking for support or inviting them to anything.

We were committed to the whole community. This is different from being committed to reaching the 'fringe' – those in the community who already show an interest in our faith or who have a family or friendship link with church members. It involves a greater openness and vulnerability, but in the long run it has more chance of being used by God. We believed prayer made a difference, and that praying for the community was one way of serving that community. While Christians do not have a monopoly on community action, prayer for the community is part of the distinctive contribution we have to offer.

Some may feel that we had low expectations. This was not the case at all. We believed that things happen when we pray, and so in one sense we were not surprised when we had opportunities to share our faith and to minister in prayer, and when we saw people become committed Christians in due time. Yet we *were* constantly surprised to discover what God was doing. We began to expect the unexpected!

Fairly early on, David visited a house where the man said, 'I'm an unbeliever, but my son would like to meet you. He's been reading the Bible.'

Wary of parents making arrangements for their teenage children, David left his number and said that of course he would go back if the son was really interested in making contact. We wanted never to seem pushy.

It turned out that the son, who was twenty at the time, was a somewhat shy young man. He had been chatting to a Christian workmate and as a result had started to read the Bible presented to him by the Gideons when he was at school. David made contact with him and we introduced him to people of his age at church. In time, faith blossomed. Today he is an active member of the church and his quiet but firm commitment to Christ stands out.

Eighteen months later, when I visited on our second 'lap' of the area, I met his parents. Despite their own apparent lack of interest in Christianity, they were thrilled at how their son had changed since he had 'got involved in the church'.

When a church engages with a community, it becomes difficult to say where evangelism ends and pastoral care begins. Some may think this ill-defined and messy. But if the church is to be effective in reaching beyond the fringe, we will have to learn to live with loose ends. The signs are that those who are not yet Christians, but who tentatively contact a community of Christians, will want to belong before they believe. They will form relationships with

Christians, and embrace the faith only when, and if, they see those Christians living it out.

We made it easy for people to say no

We made it easy for people to say 'Thanks, but no thanks!' Of course, we wanted to engage with them, but we were aware that we were on their doorstep. Their first reaction on opening the door would be mild suspicion. They might well think we were Jehovah's Witnesses or sales people. Just as dogs seem to smell fear on humans, so people seem to smell zeal on Christians, and on others who they think are out to get them. I am committed to sharing my faith with people who are ready to hear the gospel, not to imposing it on those who aren't. My responsibility is to be ready to answer anyone who asks me to account for the hope that I have, but to do so with gentleness and respect (1 Pet. 3:15).

We were not trying to open up a deep conversation on the meaning of life and the universe. We were not looking for an invitation into the home, and we were not asking for anything. We did not want to appear to be pestering people. We were making an offer, and they could take it or leave it. Either way, we were pleased to have met them, however fleetingly, for this was a contact beyond the fringe.

In our evangelism, and as we engage with people in the ebb and flow of ordinary life, we should feel more relaxed about mentioning the possibility of their not believing what we believe, or of their not wanting to learn about the faith that we love. This may seem like scoring an own goal, but I have found it to be quite the reverse. If we ourselves raise the possibility of rejecting Christianity, or of not even wanting to explore it, we show people that we live in the real world. Have you ever been cornered by someone who is an enthusiast for an obscure hobby but seems oblivious to the fact that not everyone is fascinated by it? You have – so I need not labour the point.

Jesus regularly used parables to sort out the sheep from the goats. When he announced, 'He who has ears, let him hear' (Matt. 11:15), the implication was that those who were not interested could choose not to listen. This approach highlights the fact that people have a choice to make on spiritual matters. Communicating that is in itself an important step in preparing the ground for the seed of the gospel.

We did not defend the indefensible

I mentioned earlier that in the course of visiting we unearthed some of the fall-out from a difficult period in the life of the church some twenty or more years before. There are two sides to every story, but, whatever the truth about the dispute, people had been lost from the fringe of the church. When I introduced myself as a visitor from Bitterne Church, some people would reply that they used to go there. I would try to give them an opportunity to tell me why they had left.

One woman told how she and her family had moved into the area in the 1960s from Lancashire, where her children had sung in the church choir. Soon after their move she suggested to the children that it would be good to go along to the choir practice as a way of meeting new people. Apparently, however, they were told they could not join, as their northern accents would stand out too much. The family had not been to a church since that day.

A former headmaster of a school in the city asked me outright if I would be interested to know why he longer came to church. He used to take the family to church fairly regularly. He had been deeply affected by the 1966 disaster in Aberfan in the Welsh valleys, where he had been brought up. A landslide from a colliery slag heap had engulfed the primary school, killing 144 people, mostly children. The next Sunday he had taken the family to church and had been scandalized that there had been no special prayers for those affected by the disaster. We talked at length, and though there was no startling renewal of his faith, I was heartened to see him and his wife in church some months later.

A retired teacher confided that she had been very involved in the church until her husband, who was not an active member, had died after an illness. She had been told by a member of staff that he could not offer any comfort or hope, since her husband had probably not gone to heaven. On occasions such as this, we found ourselves apologizing with tears in our eyes and praying that God would forgive his people and heal the hurts they had caused. This particular woman made her way back to church and experienced a rebirth of faith.

We were not Jehovah's Witnesses

One day a couple answered the door together, and, on seeing my dog-collar, hastily announced (genuinely, I think) that they were Jehovah's Witnesses. Without thinking I quipped, 'Role reversal!' They were not amused!

Many church leaders refuse to consider any form of door-to-door work because of the danger of being regarded as unwelcome members of a cult. So this 'territory' has been surrendered. I understand these fears. Going door to door is not everyone's gift or calling, but even so, we should not hide behind the 'JW' excuse.

Our experience was that once people realized that we were from a *bona fide* church (in our case the dear old 'safe' C of E), their relief worked in our favour. I did in fact discover some who, because of their spiritual hunger, were beginning to receive the Witnesses or Mormons into their homes. I was able to persuade some of them it would be better to meet with local Christians instead. I could not have done that from the comfort zone of my study or pulpit.

The primary reason people were receptive

The critical reason for people's receptivity is to do with the nature of God. He loves all those he has made. He does not want any to miss out on a love-relationship with him that will last for ever: 'He is patient with you, not wanting anyone to perish, but everyone to come to repentance' (2 Pet. 3:9). As we reached out to those with whom we shared the life of our community in prayer, we were in step with God's Spirit. In our desire to serve others through prayer, we had connected with God's heartbeat for his world. He is the one who has given us the gospel for others. Any response we saw, every prompting we had about which house to visit next (and there were many), every welcome and each coming to faith were all because of God. Like windsurfers, we had caught a breeze of his love and Spirit, and were simply going along with it.

Some do's and don'ts

At a workshop for our area pastors and members of their pastoral teams, we did role-plays of various door-knocking scenarios. One session descended into hilarious chaos when the door opened in response to a tentative knock, to reveal Tony, a large, bearded guy, kneeling down and pretending to be a child. He looked like a grotesque gnome as he announced in a loud voice that his mum was on the loo. Before the bewildered trainee visitor could speak, he set off to fetch her.

Situations like this do arise, and at such times our greatest need is for sanctified common sense. The following practical hints are born out of (occasionally bitter) experience. Learned technique can be off-putting. Be yourself, and ignore what is not natural for you.

Appearance

On approaching the door, remember that last-minute check. Hair and face presentable? Everything done up that should be? You do not want to give the householder any nasty surprises! For clergy, dog-collars are helpful. Be smart but casual, and make sure your face is clearly visible, especially to older people using a spy-hole.

Approach

Do not hop over low walls or flowerbeds. You are possibly being watched already. Shut gates behind you on the way in and on the way out. They will not be too thrilled with the offer of prayer if you let their beloved poodle out into the road. (Ignore this if you are confident in your ministry of raising crushed Fidos back to life!)

Look out for tell-tale signs which might be helpful in conversation. A disabled sticker on the car, the badge of an organization in the window, a child's buggy or a set of golf clubs in the porch – they are all useful clues. People like being complimented on an attractive garden, while a mess in the front may speak of some difficulty in the household.

As you approach the house, pray that God will bless this contact. Pray for any gifts you may need, but ask especially that you will be gracious and not defensive, even if you get a hostile or cold reception. One man was working up a ladder at the front of his house. He looked really put out at the prospect of being disturbed. I made a point of moving on fast, simply wishing him well as I went. He grunted. When I called again fifteen months later, God inspired me to recall the previous scenario. I kicked off by saying I remembered he had been busy last time I called, and commented that the paintwork looked good. (It did; do not gush or say something insincere.) He responded positively and was forthcoming about his needs for prayer.

Look as unthreatening as possible

Do not visit two to a door. It is good to go out in twos, but visit separate houses. If you appear as a group in one road, it looks as though you are working the place over. You are not a hit-squad! Having knocked on the door or rung the bell, stand back; do not crowd, but stay in view. Let the occupier have the high ground while you take the position of weakness. You are there to serve. You can always step forward if appropriate. Sometimes I would match a cheery welcome with a handshake, or leave with one, repeating the person's forename as I left. Only do this if it seems natural to you and to the situation.

Use positive words

I would normally say something like this: 'Hello! I'm Paul from Bitterne Church. I've just called by to say hello and to let you know that each week we pray for a couple of streets in the community. This week we're praying for you and your neighbours. We can't promise you blue skies or a winning lottery ticket, but we wondered if there was anything you wanted us to pray for. Of course, in some ways we're pleased if there's nothing, but sometimes people ask us to pray for their granny, or a friend, or even themselves.'

I say where I am from. If they are not sure which church it is, I mention the nearest pub or supermarket. That normally sorts it out. I offer my first name; they may reciprocate. By mentioning the fact that we pray for other streets I have made it clear that we have not targeted them specially because we know their cul-de-sac is a den of iniquity. We are going to pray for them anyway; it is not dependent on their decision. I link them with their neighbours; encouraging people to think about others' needs is a good thing as well as reinforcing the sense of community mentioned before. The light-hearted comment about blue skies and the lottery signals to them that we know about disappointment in life and that we are not making wild promises. Sometimes people might pick this up, and I say that we believe prayer makes a difference even though it is not always immediately obvious. This is not another example of faithlessness. It is about being honest with people.

Do not say, 'I don't think I've seen you before.' They will hear, 'You don't come to church, do you?' We are not looking to put people in a guilt trap. Some of them will be bearing guilt anyway – possibly with justification. I am sure this is another reason why some people are so obviously moved that someone is offering to pray for them. They do not feel worthy. They suspect that they have burned their boats with God, and secretly regret it.

Confidentiality

There are some neighbourhoods where the net curtains operate on automatic pilot. People may be reticent about sharing personal details with a stranger for others' consumption. If people we visited began to talk about a situation, I would stress that we did not want to be intruding on their privacy. Having asked permission to make one or two notes, I would say that we would use only a first name when praying, and that sometimes it was more appropriate to be even more discreet. Thus at the prayer service I would say, 'Someone has asked us to pray for a father who has cancer.' Often we would mention simply a 'family difficulty'. As far as possible, we used to feed the information we gathered back to the appropriate area pastor.

If you do not make a brief note with their permission, do not make the mistake of stopping on your way out to make notes by their gate. They will be very suspicious about what you are writing. Wait till you are a little way further on.

We were amazed at how open people were. When it was appropriate to go into the house – the exception rather than the rule – we would often pray then and there.

Children

If a child answers the door, immediately ask if you can speak to the grown-up in the house. Do not ask the child for prayer requests or for details about the family. If necessary, move on quickly, perhaps leaving a little note to say who called.

Calling cards

Inevitably many people will be out when you call. As your visiting progresses, you will find it helpful to visit at different times of the day and on different days of the week. We did not want to be legalistic or over-burdened by this visiting. This is important, otherwise it will quickly become a chore. We would set apart a certain time to visit, and if we ran out of time, that was that. There would always be the next time. If I had only an hour to visit, I prayed that God would lead me to the right homes.

At first I would leave my standard personal card at those homes where there was no reply. This confused people; they wondered why I had called. Had someone informed on them? Had I got bad news for them? To counter this we had some slips printed which showed the church logo and office telephone number. The slips explained why we had called and expressed the hope that they would feel free to ring if there was anything they wanted prayer for. A few did ring, but in any case it was valuable to let people know we had been. It was gratifying to discover later on that some had been sorry to miss us.

The glazier's tale

Sometimes neighbours can get in the way! One afternoon I knew that I was going to be making what could be an awkward visit. The home in question was that of a young mum who had become a Christian a year or so before, but who was unable to come to church regularly because her husband, Sean, had forbidden her to do so. Kelly was an attractive, intelligent woman who had worked as a health visitor before having their four children, the youngest of whom was just a few months old. Out of loyalty, she had never said much about Sean except that he was very opposed to Christianity. She came to services and events as and when she could, and we assured her that she should not feel guilty about not coming more. It was hard to understand how someone like Kelly could put up with such a situation.

I had just visited their next-door neighbour, a chatty woman whom I knew to be one of the organizers of the naturist sessions at the local leisure centre. I knocked at Sean and Kelly's door, and it was quickly opened by Sean. I had never met him before. I did not expect him to have two heads, but I knew I would not have a second chance to make a first impression. The last thing I needed was a neighbour sticking her nose in at this crucial moment, but before I could say anything the woman next door popped her head round and said, 'Sean, you need to talk to the vicar to fix a baptism for that baby!'

I smiled weakly and muttered something about 'that was not why I was there'. Sean and I both took cover in his front room. He had been working on his pride and joy, a large motorbike parked outside. As he wiped his hands, I constructed a sentence in which the words 'from', 'neighbour' and 'hell' featured, but not in that order. Sean responded to my attempted humour by saying she was not so bad really, and offered me a cup of tea. Kelly and the children were out. We chatted for nearly an hour; motorbikes, the police force, and double glazing all came up. As I left I said how much I had enjoyed meeting him, and to my surprise he replied that he had enjoyed chatting too.

At the prayer service the next day there was no request, just thanks for the way God had engineered my meeting with Sean. I was sure something would happen. I waited.

Some weeks later, Sean turned up at a family service with Kelly, who looked like a cat with the cream. Shortly after that, Kelly asked me to call to discuss the baby's baptism. I was happy to oblige, and on that occasion she seemed to have a lot to do in the kitchen as Sean and I talked and talked about what it meant to be a Christian. He was full of questions and listened intently. In time, it was thrilling to see Sean come to faith. He got involved in the youth club and showed he had a real heart for working with tough kids.

One day, a little later, Sean asked me to visit them again. It turned out to be one of those really moving occasions in pastoral ministry. Without much in the way of explanation, Sean got down on his knees in front of Kelly, took her hands and said how he wanted to apologize for being such a terrible husband to her over the years and for the ways in which he had let her down. We all had tears on our cheeks as I prayed for them. Soon afterwards we had a service of renewal of their wedding vows in church. 'If anyone is in Christ, there is a new creation: the old has gone, the new has come!' (2 Cor. 5:17).

Today, Sean is well on the way to qualifying as a teacher or youth worker. He has done an access course and 'A' levels, and is now doing a degree. He is a crucial figure in the youth programme and has been involved in planting a thriving daughter church. Kelly, now liberated, has played a fantastic role leading the parents and toddlers group at the church.

When I look back to my first meeting with Sean, I laugh as I realize that we cannot second-guess God. He has his own agenda!

4. Just a one-off?

A weakness of the British church, it seems to me, is the tendency to try to copy something that has worked in one place in the hope that it will produce similar results elsewhere. This aping of others' success seldom, if ever, produces lasting fruit. There is great value in learning lessons from other places, provided those lessons are tailored to the nature and needs of the second community.

I never had any intention of exporting our prayer-visiting scheme to other churches. This was because I knew that we had not invented anything special. If anything, we had turned the clock back to a time when the parson was seen about the parish along with the local bobby and the delivery men. We had not seen revival break out, although I know that a passion for prayer for those outside the church community is one of the precursors of revival. Although thrilled by the response of those in the community, I had been disappointed that larger numbers in the church had not cottoned on to what an exciting thing God was doing among us. Attendance at those prayer services rarely exceeded fifteen, even though we kept praying for fresh requests from those we were trying to reach.

A critical question is: will it work elsewhere? As I talked with colleagues around the city and further afield, they seemed to catch my enthusiasm for this approach. Its simplicity appealed; it was easy to adapt to their situations, as some of them did. Wherever people tried it, they were encouraged by the reception they got. They, too, found that people were prepared to take up a 'no strings attached' offer of prayer. Two neighbouring churches, in slightly more up-market residential areas, started to visit with similar results. Some former members of Bitterne Church, who were by now curates in a church in a run-down area of Bournemouth characterized by its bedsits, also decided to give it a try. To their surprise and mine, they also found themselves well received, but almost overwhelmed by some of the needs which came to light.

Before embarking on a visiting programme, it is good to collect census statistics and to build up as full a profile of an area as possible. You may think you have a picture of the place, but I am convinced that until you have walked the streets regularly and called at many of the homes, you cannot presume to say that you know an area.

There are many ways of developing and adapting an approach such as this. Some of the churches which have adapted it have linked prayer for the streets into their Sunday services. This has enriched those times of prayer, made the regular worshippers more aware of the needs of their community and, occasionally, encouraged those visited to come along on a Sunday.

In Bitterne we included others in the prayer-visiting, especially when we were establishing a second daughter church. Those who shared in this stage of the visiting were thrilled that people were prepared to share needs for prayer with them. We wondered whether the absence of a dog-collar would diminish the effectiveness of the contacts. They did have to explain in a little more detail who they were and where they were from. It was important to carry personal identification.

When we had visited every street in the parish, we decided to continue. If anything, this was even more fruitful. People were surprised that we had gone back. It showed we were committed to the area, and seemed to draw out a greater degree of warmth and trust.

To avoid 'visiting fatigue', it is good to take a break over a holiday period. You can set yourself whatever frequency of visiting works for you and your community. There are no rules about this. You do not have to visit when it is raining – indeed, it is not very productive to do so. Yet when we got caught in a cloudburst, people would take pity and invite us in, often with fruitful consequences.

Community prayer cells

As people become more comfortable with the idea of being prayed for, it is possible to develop your 'prayer coverage' in a number of ways. You might consider trying to establish 'prayer points' or 'houses of prayer' in each district or street. A sign displayed in the window, plus publicity via visiting, let people know that they can make their prayer requests at any time. Although they may be reticent about doing this, it does mean that the offer of prayer is there permanently, and not just when the church is praying for that street. It also establishes a prayer presence in the neighbourhood.

The best way I know of developing this idea is through 'community prayer cells' (CPCs). Drawing on lessons learned from the church in Korea, India and South America, the CPCs have been developed in Britain by Jane Holloway, who is Head of Prayer at the Evangelical Alliance. Prayer cells can operate in households, localities, workplaces or with a particular network community in mind. (See *Community Prayer Cells: How to be Good News Neighbours*, by Jane Holloway, CPAS, 1998.)

There are probably many churches which have been engaged in similar projects longer and better than ours. From people's reaction to my experience, however, I suspect that there has been a wholesale retreat from this sort of engagement with communities. This is partly because it is hard work (though to my mind incredibly rewarding), and partly because of the 'Jehovah's Witnesses syndrome' to which I have referred. But I suspect that the main reason is simply that too many church leaders and active members are over-stretched in the tasks of maintaining the church. Without realizing it, people have lost sight of the Great Commission to go into all the world with good news and to make disciples among the lost whom Jesus came to reach. Jesus told his first disciples that they would go to Jerusalem, all Judea and Samaria, and to the ends of the earth (Acts 1:8). That plainly means 'beyond their fringe'. My experience has been that to go beyond our fringe in a spirit of service and intercession leads to great openings and much fruit. Happy prayer-visiting!

PART 2

Talking with the world

TONY WATKINS

Introduction

NICK POLLARD

Angela and Bob were convinced atheists. 'Nick, we are your biggest challenge,' they would say, adding, 'but you never seem to evangelize us.'

By this they seemed to mean that I didn't try to work them over with a gospel presentation or a set of arguments every time we were together. This is what they assumed evangelism to be. They didn't think evangelism had anything to do with enjoying a beer together and chatting about films or TV programmes we had watched or books we'd read recently. This was simply friendship.

Unfortunately, some Christians seem to agree with them. I know Christians who think they are not obeying God's call to evangelism unless they are confronting people with the claims of Christ. These people are zealous for God, but I believe their zeal is misplaced.

If only people today *did* want to hear us proclaim the gospel! Some do, of course – those who are on the fringe of our churches. But few of those beyond the fringe are interested in hearing about the gospel, or want to be challenged by the claims of Christ. They *are* interested, however, in talking about the latest book or film or TV programme, even if its message is challenging – perhaps especially if its message is challenging. Most people who have seen *Schindler's List* or have read *The God of Small Things* or *Girlfriend in a Coma* will be keen to tell someone what they thought about it. People love to talk about contemporary stories which have challenged them to think deeply.

Before we talk about Jesus, or present people with his immense claims, or challenge them with the fact of his lordship, we must begin where they are. We cannot begin at square 10 if they are still at square 1. So we must be able to talk to people about the issues they want to discuss. Our task is to be able to help them to think about the spiritual and moral issues raised, and eventually to consider what Christian faith has to say about them. This makes the evangelistic process today much longer than it was even a generation ago.

Learning from Damaris

The Damaris Project takes its name from a woman who became a Christian after she heard Paul talking, in Athens, about ideas expressed by the Athenian poets (Acts 17:22–34). The Project seeks to help Christians today to get to grips with the ideas in today's culture, and to use them to communicate with the people around us.

My membership of a local Damaris study group has been vital to my ability to communicate with Angela and Bob. If I were not aware of the films they are watching, or the books they are reading, I would not be able to reach beyond the fringe to them – even if they don't realize that this is in fact part of the evangelistic process.

Talking with the world

TONY WATKINS

1. Engaging the world

The church is facing a crisis in evangelism, and it's getting deeper. The problem isn't the *amount* of evangelism; there's plenty going on (though there's scope for a great deal more). The problem is with how *effective* it is. The crisis is in our methods. We are simply not being heard.

We've all seen the solitary Christian with a big black Bible standing in the High Street bellowing his message at passers-by. The passers-by studiously ignore him, but he continues, apparently unaware that he's not getting through to anyone. I occasionally see a man standing on a milk crate and shouting into thin air. Even I don't understand what he's saying, never mind Joe Public.

We like to think we're doing a better job than that. We may be. But we may be kidding ourselves. The difference between us and the brave Bible-basher may appear much greater to us than to an outsider.

Effective evangelism

Many Christians are surprised that the Bible gives us few models of evangelism. Paul tells us that we are Christ's ambassadors (2 Cor. 5:11–21). But what does that mean in practice? What does effective evangelism look like?

The first examples that come to mind are the scary ones: Peter on the day of Pentecost (Acts 2:14–41), Paul at the Areopagus in Athens (Acts 17:22–34), and other evangelistic sermons in Acts (3:12–26; 13:14–43; 21:40 – 22:22). But read a little further and you'll find Andrew looking for his brother Simon Peter so he could tell him, 'We have found the Messiah', and take him to Jesus. Similarly, Philip invited Nathanael to meet Jesus (John 1:35–51). The Samaritan woman shared her own experience of meeting Christ (John 4:1-42). A blind man who didn't have much theology testified to the transformation in his life (John 9:1–41, esp. verse 25). Paul Harris and Phil Wall examine a couple of other approaches elsewhere in this book.

The apostle Paul told the church in Philippi that their lifestyle should mark them out:

> Do everything without complaining or arguing, so that you may become blameless and pure, children of God without fault in a crooked and depraved generation, in which you shine like stars in the universe as you hold out the word of life – in order that I may boast on the day of Christ that I did not run or labour for nothing (Phil. 2:14–16).

We, like them, are to shine like stars in the universe as we hold out the word of life. We are to hold out the good news of Jesus Christ for others to grasp. Lifestyle and words go together. People notice that there is something different about us. They may put that down to our simply being nice people, and Christians don't have a monopoly on being nice! Unless we tell them *why* we're different, how will they know?

When people become Christians, they don't buy into a lifestyle. The church is not a club for nice, well-meaning people. When people become Christians, they accept Jesus Christ as Lord. They recognize their own rebellion against him. They accept his sacrifice on their behalf as all that they need to be put right with God. And they accept his rule and authority. How can they do any of this if we do not hold the word of life out to them? God's Word, the Bible, tells us how we can know God and how we should respond to God.

What, then, are we to tell them? The gospel, of course – the good news of Jesus Christ. But what is it? Do we know it well enough to express it naturally? (People resent it when we sound like the telesales people who try to sell us double glazing in the middle of dinner.) We must get into the Bible so deeply that it gets into us and shapes all our thinking. We should know its central message inside out and be able to express it without using Christian jargon. Read it and reread it and reread it!

When I was a student I developed a habit of reading a complete book of the Bible every Sunday afternoon. My priority was the Gospels. It was brilliant for getting to know the good news better. Knowing our Bibles, however, is a means to the end (knowing God better); it is not an end in itself. If we're going to communicate the good news of Jesus Christ effectively we need to know him personally.

Shifting worldviews

How can we go on to communicate this good news clearly
and relevantly to a lost world? How do we do it? Why
does it feel so much harder now than it once did? Why is
the street preacher generally less effective these days?
Society has changed enormously in recent decades. Huge
changes are taking place at every level of society. Some of
the biggest changes are under the surface: changes in the
worldviews – the basic beliefs, values and attitudes – of the
people around us. We all have a worldview: beliefs and
attitudes to do with God, life, death, the problem with the
world, what's right or wrong. It affects our outlook on life
and almost every decision we ever make, even though
most of us aren't aware of it.

For the last 200 years, one worldview has dominated
our society above all others: the worldview known as
modernism. But over the last couple of decades everything
has changed. Modernism hasn't lived up to its promises,
but has landed us with massive problems. So most people
these days don't believe in or value the things their parents
or grandparents did; they have a new worldview, known
as postmodernism. It rejects modernism and strongly
influences almost everyone under the age of about thirty-
five (and many over thirty-five too). It is negative and
cynical. It doesn't accept anything as true. All that matters
is how it makes me feel. People are more aware again of a
spiritual side to life, though stopping well short of interest
in Jesus Christ. Society is now multicultural, and many
voices compete to offer spiritual insights.

This is not a minor change. It's the biggest shift in
outlook for over 200 years. It is a completely new way of
looking at life, the universe and everything. And the result
is that very often our evangelism doesn't hit the mark.

We now face an enormous challenge. More and more people in our culture have grown up without even a basic knowledge of Christianity. People no longer have broadly Christian values. It feels as if Christians come from a different world because we have such different beliefs and values. It is a sad fact that most people who aren't Christians aren't interested in 'straight gospel preaching'. A few people are interested in Jesus Christ; they want to know more about him or have their questions answered. But most couldn't care less. Getting them interested enough to listen to the gospel is a major task, and we don't know how to begin. Now more than ever, we need to understand others' beliefs. We need to be able to help them see the weaknesses in their worldviews. They will then be far more likely to see the relevance of Jesus Christ.

It's no longer just overseas missionaries who need skills and understanding for cross-cultural mission. Those who stay at home now need them just as much. If we are to be effective in evangelism we must understand both what makes people tick and how to communicate the gospel relevantly. Ultimately, we rely on God's Spirit to convict people. But that is no excuse for failing to communicate the good news of Jesus Christ effectively.

Ours is not just a culture of ignorance about Christian things. It's a culture of apathy. Most people have no interest in the Christian message whatsoever. They're happy as they are and can't be bothered to think about an alternative. There was a time not so long ago where you could fairly easily get into a vigorous discussion about competing claims to truth. People had views on questions like 'Is there evidence for the resurrection?' and 'Can we believe the Bible?' But now we meet indifference instead of hostility. 'It's nice that you're a Christian, but it's not really my thing.' How do we even begin to get people like this interested in hearing the good news? How do we get a hearing in our culture?

Two traps

Again and again the church has fallen into one of two traps. Either we become submerged in the surrounding culture or we cut ourselves off from it. Somehow we have to walk a tightrope between these two.

The trap of conforming to the culture in which we live is obvious. We know that the world is an ungodly place. We know that those around us are rebels against God and that they express that rebellion in all kinds of ways. We know how we feel when we fall yet again in our walk with God. And yet for many of us the world around us still has a pull. Others may sideline us or give us a hard time because of our faith. At times like that it's tempting just to keep our heads down and blend in with everyone around us. The gospel has such a challenging dimension too. Wouldn't life be easier for us if we played down that aspect? It offends people, after all! We want others to approve of us, so we try to make ourselves likeable. We want them to see that we're relevant, in touch and cool. We don't want to put them off Jesus, do we?

All of this adds up to a strong pressure to conform to the pattern of this world. Jesus recognized that we would face pressure. Otherwise he wouldn't have warned us so strongly.

> You are the salt of the earth. But if the salt loses its saltiness, how can it be made salty again? It is no longer good for anything, except to be thrown out and trampled under foot (Matthew 5:13).

Those who would come after me must deny
themselves and take up their cross daily and
follow me. For those who want to save their lives
will lose them, but those who lose their lives for
me will save them. What good is it for you to gain
the whole world, and yet lose or forfeit your very
self? All who are ashamed of me and my words,
the Son of Man will be ashamed of them when he
comes in his glory and in the glory of the Father
and of the holy angels (Luke 9:23–26).

There is pressure on us to conform. But Jesus insists
that the stakes are high and that we must maintain our
distinctiveness. 'Don't live any longer the way this world
lives,' said Paul. 'Let your way of thinking be completely
changed' (Rom. 12:2, NIrV).

As soon as we lose our distinctiveness as Christians, our
evangelism is wrecked. All we'll have to offer people is a
watered-down version of the good news, sanitized by our
internal spin-doctors. Even if we still feel we have
something to say, who will listen when words and lifestyle
don't match up? Our message is a challenging one. We
must stick with it; be faithful to it. We must maintain our
confidence in its truth. We must live by it, letting it shape
our thinking and behaviour so that we are radically
different from those around us.

But if we're not careful we can fall into the opposite
trap: isolation. One of the famous Greek myths is the
story of Odysseus, who had to sail past the island of the
Sirens. They sang so sweetly that they enticed all passing
sailors to land on the island. There they would sit listening
in a field of flowers surrounded by the bones of those who
had arrived before them and had never been able to leave.
Odysseus's solution was to plug the ears of his men with

wax and have himself tied to the mast. When he heard the Sirens' song he pleaded with his men to cut him free, but they couldn't hear and just kept rowing on past, oblivious to the alluring voices.

It sounds like a good strategy for us too: plug our ears and just keep on rowing. Once we start cutting ourselves off from the world around us we stop hearing what people are saying. If we can't hear what they're saying we won't know what they most need to hear at a particular moment. But because we've distanced ourselves so much, nobody else can hear what we have to say anyway.

We isolate ourselves because we fear contamination. The result is that, while we may be ever so holy, none of it impacts on anyone outside the kingdom of God. We become self-righteous. In the end we become hypocrites, claiming that God longs for lost people to come to him but refusing to do anything about it. Again, our evangelism is wrecked.

The Pharisees of Jesus' time fell into the same trap. We always think of them as the baddies; the men in black hats. People at the time, however, thought the Pharisees were the goodies. They were the most orthodox in their belief, the most faithful in their duty, the ones who knew their Bible best, just like today's evangelicals. But they despised Jesus for mixing with 'sinners'. They maintained their purity, only to discover that the Son of God had saved his most stinging criticism for them.

Again and again, Jesus used images for himself that had a strong missionary dimension, such as the 'light of the world' and the 'good shepherd' (John 8:12; 10:11). These had their roots in the Old Testament. When Jesus said, 'I am the true vine', those listening knew that he was deliberately taking a picture of Israel and applying it to himself (John 15:1; Ps. 80:8; Is. 5:1–7). (The temple had a golden vine over the main entrance.) The vine was a missionary metaphor. The purpose of a vine is to produce grapes. Without them the plant is not only dull but also useless. God always intended Israel to be a blessing to the surrounding nations. They were to see Israel's fruitfulness in their relationship with God and to come to know him for themselves as a result.

Jesus was announcing that Israel had failed and that he had taken on Israel's missionary function to fulfil it perfectly. The Pharisees were part of the failure. Their agenda was to maintain their purity (and their standing in the public's eyes) and to avoid contamination. When they criticized Jesus for going to a party thrown by Levi, the former tax collector, for his friends and former colleagues, Jesus retorted, 'It is not the healthy who need a doctor, but the sick' (Luke 5:27–31). Those who become part of the true vine look outward, not inward. The family of God is a missionary family, but we'll never manage to achieve anything if we keep ourselves shut away for fear of something tainting us.

In the world but not of it

Somehow we have to balance maintaining our holiness with genuinely engaging with lost people. It's not the kind of balance achieved by compromising a bit on each side. These are not mutually exclusive options. If they were, Jesus could not have done what he did. We keep the balance by working fully in both directions. There's a real tension involved in keeping the balance, but neither aspect is negotiable. We must be uncompromising both about our distinctiveness as Christians and about understanding a world that needs Christ. This is being 'in the world but not of it' (John 17:14–19).

Bill Hybels helpfully summarizes this in the form of an equation:

$$MI = HP + CP + CC$$

MI stands for Maximum Impact. Our maximum evangelistic impact depends on three factors. The first is High Potency (HP). We must nurture our relationship with God so that we become highly potent Christians. Second, we need Close Proximity (CP). Our potency as Christians can't impact on others if we don't get close to them. Conversely, being close is no use unless we are growing in God. Finally, our witness needs some content. We need Clear Communication (CC). (Bill Hybels, *Becoming a Contagious Christian*, Scripture Press, 1994, p. 51).

We must work at our holiness. We must work at engaging with the world. My focus here is on how we engage with the world around us. It means engaging with individuals and with society in general. It also means we should engage with the worldviews that shape individuals and our society. We must think through how the gospel applies to every area of life. And we must work at communicating Christ clearly and relevantly. All this brings both practical and intellectual challenges.

Some people think that this is only for intellectuals – for bookworms and deep thinkers. It's not. Anyone can do it. The people who do it best are the people who know God best – those who immerse themselves in his Word. There is a kind of spiritual insight that comes to people who have hidden God's Word in their hearts all their lives, however educated (or not) they are. Such people put many bookish types to shame. Spiritual truth is spiritually discerned (1 Cor. 2:14), and much of it comes down to our appetite for knowing God.

If you have a good brain, however, you must use it, otherwise you're being a poor steward of what God has entrusted to you. The church in Britain has had an anti-intellectual emphasis in recent years. It has been all too easy to strip the good news of its content, leaving only our spiritual experience in its place. We have not thought hard enough about our faith and how it relates to our culture. We must. There are too many people in our culture who not only do not know Christ; they see no reason why they should even think about it.

How do we begin to get through to people like this? How do we shape what we need to say? How do we avoid both compromise and isolation and keep our evangelism effective? Before we can answer that question, we need to look at how the Bible itself maintains the balance between these two dangers.

2. A biblical foundation

Jesus' last command before returning to the Father was to 'go and make disciples of all nations' (Matt. 28:19–20). This is our Great Commission. It should be our consuming passion. But Jesus didn't tell us simply to preach the gospel. Our task is to turn unbelievers into fully committed followers of Jesus Christ. How do we do thisss in practice? The Bible must be our guide. We will see that it engages with the world's beliefs, values and attitudes and presents a powerful alternative to them.

The Bible in its cultures

In the Old Testament, Israel had distinctive beliefs about God. These beliefs transformed (in theory) their whole way of life, including their relationship with other nations.

The first chapter of the Bible is a good example. It was written when Mesopotamia dominated that part of the world. People often point to links between contemporary myths and Genesis. They claim that the writer(s) of

Genesis based it on the *Atrakhasis Epic*, *Enuma Elish*, and other ancient myths. But actually Genesis is engaging with their ideas and correcting them. It directly attacks bad Babylonian theology.

It affirms that there is one God, not many (Gen. 1:1). It affirms that God is the creator of everything and that he created by the power of his word (1:1, 3). Compare that with the Babylonian gods, who had to struggle to make the world after defeating the sea monsters (representative of chaos). Genesis even goes so far as to tell us that God created the sea monsters (1:21). It insists that God created the sun and moon to serve us; they are not gods to be worshipped. Genesis doesn't even give them their names; they're just lights (1:14–19). This great chapter also asserts that humans are the pinnacle of God's creation, made in his image (1:26–30). For the Babylonians, humans were an afterthought of the gods who wanted servants to supply their needs. The Hebrews needed to get all this clear because false beliefs like these were all around them.

Much later the Babylonians carted Daniel off into exile (Dan. 1:1–7). They forced him to take a course at Babylon University in preparation for a new (compulsory) career in the Babylonian Civil Service. They were to be indoctrinated with Babylonian beliefs and practices. Nebuchadnezzar's strategy was to strip away their cultural identity and make them faithful to him and his gods.

Right from the start, Daniel and his friends took a firm stand against certain elements of the culture in which they found themselves. But they also got stuck into the pagan literature, science (all expressed in terms of magic and astrology) and other learning that they were expected to take on board. They weren't going to keep their heads down and do the minimum to get by. Nor were they going to submit to Nebuchadnezzar's plan to turn them into good Babylonians. They excelled at their studies to such an extent that Nebuchadnezzar 'found them ten times better than all the magicians and enchanters in his whole kingdom' (1:20). This was the pattern of their lives from then on. They engaged with the culture but maintained their distinctiveness. Daniel rose to be 'chief of the magicians, enchanters, astrologers and diviners' (5:11), a job title that we feel distinctly uncomfortable about. He must have been able to affirm some parts of the culture to do this. But he continued to take a clear stand against other parts of it into his old age – even at great personal risk (chapter 6).

The Bible reveals a similar pattern the whole way through. Not everybody in it had to struggle with this issue in the same way as Daniel. Rather, the Bible itself is walking the tightrope between engaging and keeping distinct. As we saw, it has a dual function: to enable us to know God and how to respond to God. Our response must involve our mind, emotions and will – our whole being.

The Bible doesn't deal with either of these aspects by giving us abstract propositions. It doesn't just give us stark statements of belief. Instead, God chose to reveal himself at certain times in history and in particular places. His Word comes to us via three specific languages (Hebrew, a little Aramaic, and Greek) and through the eyes of individuals with particular cultural outlooks. Compare this with Islamic, Hindu and Buddhist writings that are largely independent of some or all of these cultural specifics.

The Bible in our culture

The Bible negatively evaluates many aspects of the cultures

within which it was written (e.g. Amos 3). But there are some positives too (e.g. Rom. 2:14–15). Whether positively or negatively, God himself used the raw material of cultures to reveal himself to us. He even went so far as to step into one specific culture as a human being. He was 'made like his brothers and sisters in every way, in order that he might become a merciful and faithful high priest in the service of God, and that he might make atonement for the sins of the people' (Heb. 2:17).

We must somehow relate God's Word to other cultures at other times, in other places and through other languages. Sometimes it's easy (e.g. 1 Cor. 13). Sometimes it's really hard: a passage like 1 Corinthians 8 doesn't immediately apply to most of us in western society.

How can we make Scripture 'zing and sting' (in D. A. Carson's memorable phrase) if we don't know how those we're trying to reach relate to its various aspects? How will we know how they do this unless we're familiar with their culture?

When their worldview is similar to ours we do this almost instinctively. Older generations in the West grew up with a broadly Christian worldview, even if they rejected it. When I did my teacher training, a friend and I shared a flat. In the flat above lived a man named Harry, who was in his sixties. He had long since rejected Christianity, but knew lots about it. There was plenty of common understanding that enabled us to have long conversations.

But the further a worldview is from ours, the harder evangelism gets. Evangelism among younger generations is a different ball game from a couple of decades ago. They have no Christian background. My wife, Jane, used to be a primary-school teacher. Some time ago she took a group of children to their local parish church. One of the children was awestruck at this building, so unlike anything he'd ever experienced before. 'Wow!' he exclaimed, 'This is a nice palace. Who lives here?'

If we want to reach a culture, we need to understand it. And to understand it properly we need to enter into it in some way. This is what God himself has done. Jesus gave up all the glory and holiness of heaven to get deeply involved with humanity. Even the best specimens of humanity are bad enough, let alone the prostitutes, swindling tax collectors and other assorted 'low life' for whom he seemed especially concerned.

This involvement is basic to all missionary work. It's never enough simply to read books about something; you need personal experience. We've accepted that this is true for cross-cultural missionaries for years. The big difference now is that evangelism to many British people is also cross-cultural. Many in our churches haven't yet caught on to this reality. It's time we did. D. A. Carson writes: 'As much of Western culture increasingly distances itself from its Judeo-Christian roots, the task of evangelism takes on the overtones of a missionary enterprise to an alien culture: part of the task is now bound up with understanding that culture' (*The Gagging of God*, Apollos, 1993, p. 491).

We don't have the luxury of being able to preach a 'simple' gospel any more. People are biblically illiterate; they don't understand the Bible and don't want to. And they are on the way to an eternity without Christ.

Luke records five major evangelistic messages in Acts. In four of these the audience was Jewish and therefore biblically literate. Peter twice addressed Jewish crowds in Jerusalem (2:14–41; 3:12–26). Paul addressed Jews in Pisidian Antioch (13:14–43) and in Jerusalem (21:40 – 22:22). These audiences needed to see how Jesus was the fulfilment of all they believed. This has some parallels with the situation of thirty years ago when evangelism involved communicating to people who knew the Scriptures.

Paul in Athens

The fifth major evangelistic message is the one to the Council of Athens in Acts 17:16–43. This is the only significant evangelistic message addressed to Gentiles that Luke records for us. Until this time, Paul had always gone to the synagogues to reason with the Jews and the God-fearing Gentiles. He did the same in Athens. But Luke makes very little of this. Instead his focus is on Paul's discussions in the market-place. Here his main audience knew nothing of the Old Testament. Paul needed different tactics to relate the gospel to them.

Paul had time on his hands. He'd left Berea quickly, having almost provoked yet another riot (17:1–5). Now he had to wait some days for Silas and Timothy to join him. Despite his habit of being at the centre of riots, Paul didn't keep his head down, catch up on sleep or walk the tourist trail. He went to the synagogue as usual. But he also sat in the market-place day after day, talking with people there. In particular he disputed with some Epicurean and Stoic philosophers. Philosophy in those days didn't have the kind of highly intellectual and obscure feel that it has today. Philosophy was a way of life. Your philosophy was what you lived by, your worldview. The Epicurean and Stoic philosophies were the main worldviews in Athens at the time.

Paul felt 'greatly distressed' to see how much idolatry there was (17:16). He couldn't just let this go by. So he rolled his sleeves up, found a good spot and got stuck into conversations with others there. Paul's talk of Jesus and the resurrection provoked plenty of interest. Before long, the Areopagus (the council of Athens that met on the Areopagus, i.e. Mars Hill) wanted him to explain his teaching to them.

Paul started by commenting that the Athenians were very religious (or 'superstitious'; Paul may have intended both meanings), and used as his example their altar to 'an unknown god' (17:22–23). Paul could have spotted this altar in strolling around the city. But notice that he says he 'looked carefully' at the objects of worship. He was not a casual observer, but was alert to potential bridges for the gospel. Paul could have used any one of a number of starting-points. He could have launched straight into explaining why he was talking about Jesus and the resurrection to anyone who'd listen. But he chose this particular opening because then he could root his message in his listeners' worldview. That way he could get their attention in order to build a new worldview. He then worked through the doctrine of God and the doctrine of humanity and finished with a call to repentance.

What Luke recorded for us is just a brief summary of Paul's speech. It takes under two minutes to read it aloud. Paul would undoubtedly have gone on for much longer (this was the man who spoke for so long on another occasion that Eutychus nodded off and fell out of a window). I once read that speeches in the Areopagus were often three or four hours long. Along the way, Paul quoted Greek poets and philosophers. The most obvious examples are the two quotations in verse 28: 'For in him we live and move and have our being' (from Epimenides the Cretan) and 'we are his offspring' (from Aratus). It is almost certain that Paul used others during the course of his message. In fact, there are likely references to five others (Euripides, Plato, Posidonius, Cleanthes and Aeschylus) even in the summary Luke has given us.

Paul was picking up on points where these Greek writers had got it right. They may not have had a biblical background, but that doesn't mean their thinking was completely up the spout. Just because people are not converted doesn't mean that they think only rubbish. Paul's hearers were people made in the image of God who were asking serious questions about life, the universe and everything. They were also finding some answers because, being in God's image, they had access to some truth (Rom. 1:18–23). The Epicureans had some things right; the Stoics had other things right. Paul takes the trouble to affirm these things.

This is a 'powerful apologetic device that enables Paul to base himself on acceptable Greek theistic assumptions while at the same time going beyond them' (Alister McGrath, *Bridge-building*, IVP, 1992, p. 49). Paul 'knows the importance of establishing as much initial common ground as possible with his hearers' (F. F. Bruce, *The Acts of the Apostles*, rev. ed. Apollos, 1990, p. 382). What was Paul doing here? Was he trying to make his hearers think that there wasn't much difference between him and them? Or that he went along with everything these Greek writers said? Not at all. But 'if men whom his hearers recognised as authorities had used language which could corroborate his argument, he would quote their words, giving them a biblical sense as he did so' (F. F. Bruce, *Paul: Apostle of the Free Spirit*, Paternoster, 1977, p. 242).

Paul was also careful to refute some of the Epicurean and Stoic beliefs. The resurrection is the major example. The people of Athens didn't believe resurrection was possible. In a play by Aeschylus, about the court of the Areopagus, Apollo says, 'Once dead, there is no resurrection.' Everyone believed this. It's this Athenian conviction that resurrection wasn't possible that lies behind verse 18, where they understand Paul's talk of Jesus and the resurrection to mean two gods, Jesus and Anastasis (Greek for 'resurrection'). Since resurrection doesn't happen, Anastasis must be the name of god who offers a fresh start in life.

Where and when did Paul learn all this Greek poetry and philosophy? Did he simply quote what he'd picked up while chatting to people in the market-place? If so, he certainly didn't pick it up casually; Paul had 'looked carefully' at the objects of worship. He also debated with the philosophers; it was not idle chat. Paul listened carefully to what was said and genuinely engaged with it both in the market-place and in the Areopagus.

Could he be quoting from material he had known since his youth? Before his conversion Paul was a Pharisee. It's hard to imagine him reading Greek poets then! But Paul was brought up a Roman citizen as well as a Jew, so it is just possible that he grew up reading Greek writers.

Or had he been purposefully studying them for years? I think this is most likely. Paul was the 'apostle to the Gentiles'. He was always ready to be 'all things to all people so that by all possible means I might save some' (1 Cor. 9:22). Surely he would have wanted to understand the cultures of the Gentiles he was striving to win for Christ.

How Paul got to know Greek culture so well doesn't matter much. The fact that he did so matters very much indeed. The point is that Paul was familiar with both the ideas and the details of Greek writers. He knew them well enough to do more than lob some everyday saying into his speech so that he could appear relevant. He knew them well enough to engage with the ideas seriously, respectfully and yet critically. He understood the culture well enough to take his thoroughly biblical message and express it in the thought forms, ideas and phrases that were part and parcel of that culture. He understood where his listeners were coming from well enough to move at least some from complete ignorance to faith.

Did Paul regret it?

But does Paul, as some people have suggested, then backtrack on this approach when he gets to his next stop, Corinth? Was his approach in Athens a mistake? Is this why only a few were saved? Is this why he wrote what he did in the opening chapters of 1 Corinthians?

> Where are the wise? Where are the scholars? Where are the philosophers of this age? Has not God made foolish the wisdom of the world? For since in the wisdom of God the world through its wisdom did not know him, God was pleased through the foolishness of what was preached to save those who believe ... God chose the foolish things of the world to shame the wise ... When I came to you, brothers and sisters, I did not come with eloquence or superior wisdom as I proclaimed to you the testimony about God. For I resolved to know nothing while I was with you except Jesus Christ and him crucified. I came to you in weakness and fear, and with much trembling. My message and my preaching were not with wise and persuasive words, but with a demonstration of the Spirit's power, so that your faith might not rest on human wisdom, but on God's power (1:20–21, 27; 2:1–5).

Not at all. There are several reasons why we can be sure of this.

1. Paul's commitment to preaching nothing but Christ isn't new. Paul *always* did this. What was the heart of his message in Athens? 'Jesus and the resurrection.' The difference lay in how he presented his material, not in what the material was.

2. 'Nowhere in either Acts or Corinthians does Paul indicate any repentance or even regret over what he did on Mars Hill. This is reading into the text what simply is not there,' writes Norman Geisler (*The Need for Defending the Faith*, Southern Evangelical Seminary website, 1997; http://ses.digiweb.com/whyapol.htm).

3. In a subsequent letter to the Corinthians, Paul describes his ministry as 'demolishing arguments and every pretension that sets itself up against the knowledge of God' (2 Cor. 10:5). This is exactly what he was doing in Athens.

4. Paul must have preached 'Jesus Christ and him crucified' or his talk of resurrection and judgment would have meant nothing. It just isn't spelt out in the summary we have. Paul may have spent more time on the resurrection because Athenians didn't believe it was possible.

5. Paul was experienced in evangelism in the Gentile world by this time. His decision at Corinth would have been based on his assessment of the situation there. It was the administrative capital of the region and had a very unsavoury reputation. At the time, 'to play the Corinthian' meant to be sexually immoral. A place like that needed a different emphasis. This also explains Paul's going to them in 'weakness and fear and much trembling'.

6. Someone so experienced in evangelism would not change his tactics just because only a few people were

converted. We jump easily to this conclusion because we are so 'numbers-oriented'. We want to see lots of professions of faith. Sometimes it seems our credibility as churches hangs on it. This was not Paul's outlook, since it's not a biblical criterion of success (cf. Matt. 7:13–14).

7. How can Paul's attempt to reach the thinkers of Athens be called a failure? Think how far back his audience was starting in their knowledge of the God of the Bible. It's incredible that *any* became Christians as a result of Paul's brief stay in the city and one address to the Areopagus. Luke tells us that some believed. Among them were Damaris and Dionysius. We know nothing more about Damaris, but church tradition tells us that Dionysius, who was a member of the Areopagus, became the first bishop (or overseer) of Athens, and there is no reason to doubt this.

Although Paul used ideas from Greek culture quite happily, then, he never compromised his message. He didn't get sucked into Greek culture, but used what he could of it, affirming truth and denying error whenever it was appropriate. When Paul wrote his second letter to Corinth, the church there was attacking him. Some members thought that Paul and his team lived 'by the standards of this world'. His reply is significant:

... though we live in the world, we do not wage war as the world does. The weapons we fight with are not the weapons of the world. On the contrary, they have divine power to demolish strongholds. We demolish arguments and every pretension that sets itself up against the knowledge of God, and we take captive every thought to make it obedient to Christ (2 Cor. 10:3–5).

We live in a post-Christian culture, full of arguments and pretensions that set themselves up against the knowledge of God. Paul says they need to be demolished. Thoughts – ideas – must be made obedient to Christ. In the context, Paul can't be talking primarily about personal holiness, which is how we generally apply this verse, but 'cultural holiness'. When ideas are in accordance with Scripture they can be affirmed. When they are not, they must be brought into line.

3. How do we engage with people in practice?

Have you ever had one of those conversations when you know you ought to be able to bring in a Christian perspective? The only problem is how. As the conversation goes on you become more and more anxious. You know you *should* say something but you just can't think what. Probably all of us have been there at some time or other. What can we do about it?

Guiding conversations

Think about when this happens. What kind of conversations are they? I think they fall into three main groups.

1. *Personal issues.* When something significant happens in someone's life, he or she may well talk about it. It could be something terrible like bereavement or divorce. It may be something exciting – a birth or a marriage. Or perhaps something less tangible – a sense of hopelessness or anxiety about the future. When such issues come up in

conversation, there are plenty of things we can say as Christians, including, as Paul Harris says in Part 1, 'Can I pray for you?' The gospel speaks powerfully into these situations.

2. *Issues in society*. We have many openings for presenting a Christian angle on wider issues in society. As Christians we should have something to say on youth crime, homelessness, treatment of single parents, and so on. Big issues of life find their way into our conversations. But often all we do is share the same gloominess as everyone else.

I remember all too well a conversation I had with my barber some time ago. Screen violence and its effects on society were in the news and we got talking about it. I may have said one or two helpful things, but the door was wide open for me to bring a distinctively Christian perspective. I could have talked about God's view of violence. I could have talked about why people make violent films in the first place and what it betrays about their hearts. I could have talked about the consequences of our becoming anaesthetized to violence by seeing so much of it. But I didn't. I bottled out and we both just shook our heads in despair at our society. One day we'll come back to this issue and this time I'll be ready.

3. *Issues in the media*. This one is perhaps less obvious. These are the conversations about what's been on TV, the film we've just seen or the book we're reading. People talk about these things all the time. Nobody thinks it's odd or 'heavy' if we bring them up in conversation. The problem we have is that our conversations about the film we've just watched are often so trivial.

'I went to see *The Truman Show* last night.'

'Oh, really? Any good?'

'Yes, it was pretty good. We got there early, though, and

the fleapit of a cinema treated us to fifteen minutes of country and western music. It was dire!'

'We had *Blondie's Greatest Hits* at the multiplex when I went to *Saving Private Ryan*. I hadn't heard that stuff in years. It was great! And I love the seats there. Have you tried the luxury ones yet?'

Great conversation! Keep that up and you'll have plenty of opportunities to make the other person think. Or not!

We need to remember that what we read and watch and listen to carries many messages. Every book or film is written out of a particular worldview. The writer or director may or may not have been conscious of it. Sometimes it's obvious. The astronomer Carl Sagan's books, both fiction and non-fiction, were always clearly anti-Christian. Sometimes the worldview is almost impossible to pin down. But it's there nonetheless.

These messages, these worldviews, influence us. It may be a slow, subtle process like the constant dripping of an outside tap wearing away the stone beneath it. Imagine the drip-fed influence of *EastEnders* when you've watched it two or three times a week for years. What does that do to your ideas of morality? If this doesn't work, if the media don't influence us over time, why are such massive sums spent on advertising? Sometimes the influence may be sudden and strong. How many people came out of *Schindler's List* without being profoundly affected?

Every day we are bombarded with messages from all the media. We get up and listen to the news and perhaps read the paper over breakfast. The post brings a pile of junk mail, a magazine and newsletters from various charities. On our way to work we pass dozens of billboards. (Count them one day and then watch to see how often they change the posters.) At work there's a whole raft of new messages to contend with. Over lunch, perhaps we do some shopping and get presented with hundreds of brand names and products. On our way home we might listen to a commercial radio station for the travel news. After work we perhaps put our feet up and watch the box. Maybe a little web-surfing later on. How many adverts have we been exposed to? How many other things have we read, watched and listened to that are all communicating to us?

Gradually, people build their worldview from all these messages. We start out with a worldview inherited from our parents. At school it may begin to change as teachers and friends bring other influences to bear on us. And as we grow up and receive more and more messages from the media, so our worldview gradually transforms into something which may be quite different from that which we started with.

The messages we receive may or may not be consistent with Christianity. Some will have a positive influence and some will be negative. No prizes for guessing which way *Chariots of Fire* and *Pulp Fiction* influenced people.

There is enormous scope for having very constructive conversations with people that relate to the media. Our biggest challenge is to get away from the trivia. If I'd got chatting with someone who wasn't a Christian after watching *Saving Private Ryan* it would have been easy to have talked about the idea of sacrificing oneself for others. We would probably have discussed the rights and wrongs of the Second World War and war in general. The Bible has plenty to say on such issues, and such a conversation would not have seemed strained.

There is obviously some overlap between the three areas of conversation that I've outlined. Personal issues often arise out of what happens in the wider society. And books, films, music and TV are always dealing with the same kinds of issues, often with some particular angle on them.

Of course, there are other types of conversation too. I am convinced that the gospel has something to say about everything. However, it's not always easy to make the connection without coming across as rather false. If you link the gospel to a friend's recent fishing trip you're likely to sound a little corny. Some people could get away with it, but it would seem very cheesy if I tried it.

Some conversations lend themselves, then, to bringing in a Christian dimension. But what then? It's all very well knowing that this is the kind of conversation where we may have an opportunity. The question, is how do we develop it?

There are three important factors to work on if we want to get better at this.

Know the gospel

It is vital to know the gospel well. We have no excuse for not knowing what we believe. We are Christ's ambassadors (2 Cor. 5:20). Would any ambassador not know his or her country's foreign policy? If Louis de Bernières's portrayal in *Captain Corelli's Mandolin* is historically accurate, the Italian ambassador to Greece during the Second World War was totally ignorant of Mussolini's intention to invade Greece. This points to the craziness of Mussolini's actions, because we know that ambassadors aren't generally kept in the dark. They know what's going on. And they don't hesitate to stand up for their country when there is an international incident.

God has entrusted to us the ministry of reconciliation (2 Cor. 5:18–20). We need to know how that reconciliation comes about. Learning a gospel outline is helpful. These are best used as a framework for what we need to say, not for reciting parrot-fashion. *Two Ways to Live*,

Bridge to Life, and similar outlines are extremely useful tools to help us in our evangelism. But they cannot substitute for knowing the good news of Jesus Christ well enough to communicate it clearly and simply. It's not just the core of the gospel we need to know. We need to get to know all of God's Word better. The gospel is central to the whole Bible. We need to understand Jesus' life, death and resurrection in the context of the whole of God's revelation.

We also need to know God's Word better so that we can identify the Christian response to issues. That's not to say that the Bible directly addresses every issue that we come across. It doesn't say anything specific about genetic engineering or western democracies, for instance. As we get to know God better through meeting him in his Word, however, we will develop a sense of which principles relate to these questions.

Know what's going on

Christians should be up on current events. We should think about what the gospel has to say to those situations. We need to demonstrate genuine, godly compassion for a world in a mess, arising out of God's great compassion for us. We can't go to every situation and help, but we can pray and give. We should read our newspapers on our knees – and not because the broadsheets are unmanageable any other way.

We should also be aware of the current events in the lives of our friends and colleagues. I'm not suggesting we should pry into their lives. Nor should we get involved in gossip so that we know what's going on. But we should be taking time to get to know people. We should have the time to ask how they are, and to listen to their response.

We should be alert for signs that all is not well, and demonstrate Christ's care for them.

When we meet others, the big issues of the day and the big issues of personal life do come up in conversation. Whether it be yet more conflict in the Balkans, a scandal involving a public figure or ongoing trauma with a rebellious teenager, we are likely to discuss it with our friends. If we are ignorant and indifferent to these things, we do no-one any favours. But if we are genuinely concerned and have a real compassion for those who are caught up in these situations, it shows through. And when it does so, people have a small glimpse of the compassion of God.

Know people's beliefs and values and where they get them

We have seen how Paul understood the beliefs that were under the surface of the culture of Athens. When he talked to people he genuinely engaged with their ideas. He affirmed some aspects of their worldview as having some truth. But there was also error, and Paul ensured that he exposed it. He showed that there were weaknesses in what they believed and then went on to talk about Jesus. His evangelism was true to God's Word. It was also relevant to their culture.

In our society people don't sit around in the marketplace discussing their ideas about life; they sit in the pub or the canteen at work. They don't tend to read much philosophy and poetry. They read novels and magazines. They watch films and TV. They listen to popular music and surf websites. These are the sources from which most people pick up large chunks of their basic beliefs and attitudes.

We need to understand others' beliefs. We should also understand where and how they get them. We need to be aware of the messages people receive from what they watch and read. And we must be able to show them why those messages are poor substitutes for the good news of Jesus Christ. As long as they're happy with the worldviews they already have, they won't want to listen. But if we can help them begin to see the weaknesses, they will begin to understand that they need the gospel.

Hannah was a student at a conference at which I was speaking. She told me about her housemate, who was trying to base her life on the ideas in James Redfield's books. His first, *The Celestine Prophecy* (Bantam, 1994), purports to be the story of the discovery of an ancient Peruvian manuscript (written in Aramaic, which is how they know it was genuine. Eh?). This manuscript contains nine insights for living life to the full. It's very spiritual, some of the early insights seem to make a lot of sense, it's attractive and it addresses some of the needs we're aware of. But, while there's plenty in it we can affirm, at the end of the day it's New Age thinking that will leave its followers living out a lie.

Hannah and I talked about the ideas in the book and some of the problems with them. For one thing, it doesn't have any concept of the sinfulness of human beings. Any worldview that doesn't allow for this is going to end up as a big disappointment when it can't really explain why things keep going wrong in our lives. One day Hannah's friend will discover that while she might feel more relaxed or energized, she's still the same person with a load of guilt that needs to be dealt with. As we talked through James Redfield's ideas, it was clear to us that while they addressed real needs, only the gospel could adequately deal with them because only the gospel deals with that fundamental problem of our rebellion against God. I hope Hannah was able to have a similar conversation with her friend afterwards.

We often read the same books and watch the same programmes as some of our friends, neighbours and colleagues. If we've thought hard about them we have more chance of being able to relate the gospel to them when they come up in conversation.

Some time ago Jane and I went to a friend's house for dinner. A colleague of our friend came too – a very bright professor, but not a Christian. During the evening I confessed that I'd been to see *Spiceworld the Movie* (all in the cause of understanding the culture!). He was surprised that there was anything of substance in it. I told him that I didn't think there was, really. But I went on to say that this is the point of the film. Image is everything; substance is immaterial. The film was an attempt to boost a career that was beginning to decline. It showed the Spice Girls as being young, fun and cool; people who love their music but don't take it or anything else ·seriously – not even themselves.

We went on to have a long, serious conversation about how our society is obsessed with image and how nothing is taken seriously. We talked about hedonism, morality and the point of life. He didn't end up on his knees in repentance at the end of the evening. But we did consider some huge questions that will make a follow-up conversation with him so much easier.

But this brings us back to our tightrope. What should we read and watch and listen to? Should a Christian ever read something like Ben Elton's *Popcorn* or Helen Fielding's *Bridget Jones's Diary*? Or watch a film like *Spiceworld the Movie* or *The Shawshank Redemption*? Should we go to a lecture by Richard Dawkins? Some

Christians reply with a resounding 'No'. They're concerned, rightly, that Christians should not conform to the culture. The world should notice that we have different standards. They remind us that we may be in the world but we are definitely not of it.

But we mustn't isolate ourselves, either. As we've seen, both conforming and isolation wreck evangelism. If people are to hear our message, we must speak it relevantly and engagingly. We cannot afford to be ignorant of what shapes our listeners' most basic beliefs and attitudes. What they read, watch and listen to influences them. So, to understand the people, we must understand how these things do influence them. Then we must be able to engage with them at a suitable level. We need to start where people are at and build a case for why they need to consider Christ. Too often we don't do that. Why? We don't know what the right starting-points are. We don't know how to catch people's attention. We don't understand their worldviews well enough to recognize their problems. We must recognize when someone is asking the right questions or is groping towards some answers. And we must also perceive and challenge wrong answers and wrong perspectives on life.

Andy works with students in a Damaris study group. At one of the group meetings, they had been discussing Douglas Coupland's book, *Girlfriend in a Coma* (Flamingo, 1998). Afterwards, Andy went to the university Students Union where he got into conversation with a student who wasn't a Christian. The student told Andy that he was reading a great book called *Girlfriend in a Coma* which was asking the same kinds of questions as he himself was. Is there a meaning to life? What is it? Is the world a place of hopelessness, or is there something that can give us hope? Is there such a thing as The Truth? Andy had a great conversation because these are the kinds of questions that the good news of Jesus Christ answers clearly. The big opening came because Andy had read and thought hard about the same book as the student.

So it's OK for Christians to read and watch what others are reading? Well, yes and no. Of course we must watch our life and doctrine closely, and that will rule out reading some things and watching others. But at the same time it is, at least to some extent, a vital task for anyone who longs to see the gospel really hitting home.

It's important to remember that we're not talking about the really offensive material that's out there. What we need to engage with is the normal, everyday stuff of culture that people, including ourselves, read and watch as a matter of course. Most of us read newspapers. Most of us sit in front of the box and watch the same things as our friends. We read many of the same books. We go to watch the same films. We rent many of the same videos. We listen to the same music. And just like our friends we do it all for entertainment.

What I'm saying is that we should start thinking about all the messages that come into our brains and those of our friends day after day. We need to evaluate these messages, for the sake of both our discipleship and our evangelism. The vast majority of the influential ideas come through sources that we wouldn't struggle with very much.

Having said that, though, some material is more problematic. I am not suggesting that we should all start reading and watching unhelpful things for the sake of the gospel. Francis Schaeffer once gave a lecture on Henry Miller and was asked afterwards, 'But are you saying that we've all got to read these dirty books?' Schaeffer replied, 'No, but some of you have got to.' At least some people within the church need to evaluate some things on behalf of the rest of us. And there are some things that we know enough about before we start that we leave well alone.

Not all Christians needed to see *Spiceworld*, but some did, because that's the world of those we are trying to reach. Not everyone needs to engage seriously with Richard Dawkins, but some of us do if he's influential among our friends and colleagues. *Someone* needs to read and watch and understand because these things shape the culture we live in now. Whether through being acute observers and listeners of those around us, or through careful study, we must know how to respond to the beliefs, ideas and values of our friends, colleagues and neighbours.

Double listening

John Stott, in his marvellous book *The Contemporary Christian* (IVP, 1992), writes of the need for Christians to engage in 'double listening'. Let me quote one section at length.

> How, then, can we be both conservative and radical simultaneously, conservative in guarding God's revelation and radical in our thoroughgoing application of it? How can we develop a Christian mind, which is both shaped by the truths of historic, biblical Christianity, and acquainted with the realities of the contemporary world? How can we relate the Word to the world, understanding the world in the light of the Word, and even understanding the Word in the light of the world? We have to begin with a double refusal. We refuse to become either so absorbed in the Word, that we escape into it and fail to let it confront the

world, or so absorbed in the world, that we conform to it and fail to subject it to the judgment of the Word. Escapism and conformity are opposite mistakes, but neither is a Christian option.

In place of this double refusal we are called to double listening, listening both to the Word and to the world. It is a truism to say that we have to listen to the Word of God, except perhaps that we need to listen to him more expectantly and humbly, ready for him to confront us with a disturbing, uninvited word. It is less welcome to be told that we must also listen to the world. For the voices of our contemporaries may take the form of shrill and strident protest. They are now querulous, now appealing, now aggressive in tone. There are also the anguished cries of those who are suffering, and the pain, doubt, anger, alienation and even despair of those who are estranged from God. I am not suggesting that we should listen to God and to our fellow human beings in the same way or with the same degree of deference. We listen to the Word with humble reverence, anxious to understand it, and resolved to believe and obey what we come to understand. We listen to the world with critical alertness, anxious to understand it too, and resolved not necessarily to believe and obey it, but to sympathize with it and to seek grace to discover how the gospel relates to it ...

'Double listening', however, contains no element of self-contradiction. It is the faculty of listening to two voices at the same time, the voice of God through Scripture and the voices of men and women around us. These voices will often

> contradict one another, but our purpose in
> listening to them both is to discover how they
> relate to each other. Double listening is
> indispensable to Christian discipleship and
> Christian mission (pp. 27–29).

All of this is central to what we do in the Damaris Project. This kind of thinking and studying is best done in small groups. Different insights and perspectives help everyone in the group to understand more thoroughly. A group provides motivation to read further, for the purpose of understanding, not just enjoyment. It helps people think how to apply what they have learnt in their evangelism. And it brings a vital pastoral dimension as members pray for and support each other. That is useful when studying even the most innocent of non-Christian material. With some of the more challenging material it is vital.

We also need to remember that this approach is just one aspect of evangelism. It's the Spirit of God working in people's hearts who converts them. It's not a matter of how well we understand their worldviews or how well we answer their questions. It's not even a question of how well we explain the gospel. God must take away their blindness. But that doesn't excuse us from knowing answers to tough questions, knowing the gospel inside out and doing all in our power to make God's Word bite in the lives of our listeners.

In the same way, we are not excused from knowing and understanding the beliefs and values, the worldviews and cultures of those we are trying to reach. The Bible leaves us with a tension between doing all we humanly can and yet depending totally on God to do the work. Paul knew better than any of us that it's only the Lord who saves people – yet it didn't stop him from saying, 'Since, then, we know what it is to fear the Lord, we try to persuade people' (2 Cor. 5:11).

That's why we must relate all our study of the culture around us to Scripture. It is the only solid reference point by which we can evaluate ideas. That's why we need to pray through the implications for our evangelism of what we see in the books and films we study. Studying our culture should equip us to use the Bible more effectively in our evangelism, whether preaching or personal, as we apply God's Word to key points in the worldview of those we're trying to reach. The Bible needs to bite the tender bits!

We haven't yet thought about what this looks like in practice. When we've watched a film or read a book, how do we evaluate it?

Stages in evaluation

Five stages are involved in thinking it through. It's helpful to work through the same five stages when chatting with non-Christians.

1. Identify the worldview

We need to identify what beliefs, values and attitudes underpin what we're hearing. What view of reality are we being presented with? Where is the writer or director coming from? Where is this person coming from?

The kinds of questions to ask are: What do they think is really real – just the physical world, or a spiritual dimension too? What do they believe about God? What does it mean to be human? What is the point of life? What happens when we die? What is right and wrong? How do we know? How do we know anything at all?

What is the problem with the world, and what's the solution? (A useful book about current worldviews is James Sire's *The Universe Next Door*, IVP, 3rd edn, 1997.)

Identifying the worldview (and the other steps below) is not just for a Damaris study group or when you're particularly trying to understand a certain film or book. It should be something that we do constantly. Do you ever ask yourself about the values you see portrayed in *Casualty* or *EastEnders*? Do you ever stop to identify the priorities for life that advertisers are pushing at you?

The Truman Show contains many links with Christian ideas. Truman Burbank is the unwitting star of a television show that runs twenty-four hours a day and is broadcast all over the world. Truman had been adopted at birth by the television company and had grown up constantly filmed by secret cameras. Everyone in Truman's life is an actor. Only he doesn't know. The town he lives in is in fact inside a huge studio.

One day Truman has a 'Damascus road' experience. He sees the light quite literally when a stage light drops out of the 'sky' in front of him with the name of a star painted on its side. Other slips in the management of the set make him suspect that life is not all it seems. Eventually he tries to escape by sailing off in a boat, the *Santa Maria*. After arranging a fearsome storm to dissuade Truman from his escape attempt, the director of the show, Christof, speaks to him from the sky. He tells Truman that he is the creator of the world that Truman knows, and that he has cared for Truman and has provided a safe environment for him. Truman is unimpressed – his whole life has been a sham; everything about him has been manipulated for the benefit of others. His 'reality' has been nothing but an illusion.

Some of the Christian links are obvious. Christof's name is not an accident. He is as God to Truman – a connection made more explicit by Christof's declaration of himself as the creator. But is this use of Christian ideas positive or negative? It is overwhelmingly negative. Christof's control centre is behind the moon in the roof of the set: the creator is the man in the moon. Christof is not a benevolent character but a manipulator. The environment he has made for Truman may be safe, but it is a deception; he has done all he can to prevent Truman from knowing the truth.

It seems clear that Andrew Niccol, the writer and director, sees God (or the idea of God) in the same way. If there is a God, he must be a despot. Maybe, suggests Niccol, the life we live is not the 'real reality', but is based on a lie because of its Judeo-Christian origins. We must escape to another reality, one without the man in the moon. It's a message of the human spirit triumphing over circumstances to achieve freedom. The same message comes out in a different way in Niccol's earlier film *Gattaca*.

The Matrix, written and directed by Andy and Larry Wachowski, also explores the idea that there might be an altogether different reality behind what we assume is normal life. Again, there are many Christian links and it's clear that the Wachowski brothers are not Christians. But they do seem to understand Christianity and to be sympathetic towards it. This time the Christian imagery is used for the good guys.

Identifying the worldview isn't just a matter of looking for links with Christian ideas and seeing if they are used positively or negatively. But it's a good start. Whenever you read a novel, watch the TV or listen to an album, ask yourself, 'What are they really saying about life? Where are they coming from?'

2. Analyse the worldview

Having identified the beliefs, values and attitudes that are being communicated (or that shape the communication), we need to explore them a little more. Somehow we seem to think that it's the Christians' role in life to answer all the tough questions while everyone else gets to ask them. We're constantly on the back foot in our evangelism, and being defensive. But we should go on the front foot and start asking tough questions of other ideas and worldviews. If we give others a chance to explore their worldviews a little more, they sometimes find that their ideas don't hang together too well. If we're considering a film, book or album, though, we will probably have to content ourselves with trying to work out for ourselves how the writer might answer the tough questions. For instance: Do the ideas hang together and make sense? Which ones do and which don't? Do these ideas actually fit with reality? Do they describe the world as it really is? Or are they a distortion or invention? Do they ignore some significant factor? Do they work? What happens if you push these ideas a little further? What kinds of tensions and difficulties might they lead to? Where does it all come crashing down?

In her book *The Whole Woman* (Doubleday, 1999), Germaine Greer reiterates something she said in her earlier book *The Female Eunuch*: men hate women. At least, all men hate some women some of the time. Many men would strenuously deny this. It should not be true of any Christian man. But is she right? Partly, yes, but she's not telling the whole story, is she? This isn't actually a gender matter. We should, in fact, extend her statement: all *people* hate at least some other *people* some of the time. It's something that's inherent in human beings since the fall:

we are not always characterized by love.

Central to Ian McEwan's novel *Enduring Love* (Vintage, 1998) is our perspective on life, especially our sense of right and wrong. The story opens with a balloonist and his grandson in difficulties as they attempt to land. The narrator, Joe, and four other men run to help. They cling to the ropes, but when a violent gust of wind suddenly blows the balloon and its human anchors over an escarpment, one of the men lets go. Now much lighter, the balloon lurches upwards and three others drop off to save themselves. One man hangs on, but finally and fatally loses his grip when the balloon gains too much height. Joe is tortured by the question of whether or not he let go first and why the men let go at all instead of hanging on.

He muses on the dilemma of whether to act altruistically or to save our own skins. McEwan says that selfishness is the 'basic moral factor about ourselves', and yet we also have this drive to co-operate. This, he says, is 'our mammalian conflict' – something we share with other mammals.

Our mammalian conflict? We need to ask some questions at this point. Where is McEwan coming from? Apparently from a strongly atheist position which results in his seeing humans as no different from any other mammal. Is the dilemma of altruism or self-interest a problem that all mammals face? It isn't anything of the sort. It is a uniquely human conflict. There are other social animals, but human altruism goes way beyond a simple instinct to protect our group.

Where would McEwan say this conflict comes from? From the pressure to survive? Does that adequately account for the strong human drive to care for others, even to sacrifice oneself for them? A Christian explanation is that we humans have this conflict because we still bear the image of God. We instinctively know that others should take precedence. Yet because we're fallen, the self wins again and again.

Whatever you're reading or watching or listening to, keep asking yourself, 'Does this all add up?' Like Paul in Athens, we can be positive when we agree and speak clearly against elements that are wrong. Every belief system, every book and film contains both truth and error.

The Yin-Yang symbol, used by Buddhists and New Agers, is meant to symbolize the idea that in all light there is a little bit of darkness and in all darkness there is a little bit of light. Is this true? Yes, in that though we are made in the image of God, we are fallen and corrupted. No, because we can't apply it to the whole of reality. 'God is light; in him there is no darkness at all' (1 John 1:5). Satan is totally evil.

3. Affirm the truth

In the course of identifying and evaluating the worldview, then, we need to keep asking: 'What is the good in this that we can happily affirm? What is consistent with a biblical Christian perspective?' The 'biblical Christian perspective' part is crucial, for we have no other reliable way of assessing the rightness or wrongness of anything that we encounter. We certainly can't trust our feelings alone.

Douglas Coupland's novel *Girlfriend in a Coma* is a powerful critique of the emptiness of modern living. We live in a hopeless society. Hope is something alien to many people today. It's not hard to see some of the causes. The years following the Second World War were a time of rising wealth and optimism; we'd 'never had it so good'. But the nuclear threat loomed ever larger. More and more environmental crises became apparent. As material prosperity grew, so did a sense of dissatisfaction. And now many people's horizons have narrowed to just their own tiny world.

Coupland's characters are exactly at this point. They have no big picture of life, and no real hope. There are fragments of immediate, personal, short-term hope, but nothing substantial (until towards the end, but I don't want to give the game away!). It is a bleak view of life, and therefore true to the way many people really feel. Like Andy, who discussed Coupland's book with a student, we can say, 'Coupland has got it right. This is what people are like.'

4. Discern the error

But we mustn't forget to keep asking: 'What is wrong in this, that we need to challenge? What is inconsistent with a biblical Christian perspective?'

Coupland has plenty to say about the spiritual dimension to life in *Girlfriend in a Coma*, but it's nothing like the Bible's portrayal of it. For Coupland, God is inaccessible, vague, remote and unknowable. Those who have died become ghosts that can interact with the living, even making them pregnant. There is no judgment. The dead, like the living, are a mixture of good and bad.

I think Coupland is experimenting with his own beliefs and thoughts in *Girlfriend in a Coma*. They're not really coherent, and he's got the wrong end of the stick altogether about the spiritual realm. But he's on the right track. At the end of the book he is sure that there is some Truth to be found. But he hasn't the foggiest what it is. He almost seems to suggest that the process of looking for the truth is more important than finding it. And he certainly has no conception that this Truth might be a personal, knowable God.

5. *Identify a response*

What is a good Christian response to these ideas? What would Jesus say in this situation?

For many people, friendship with Christians is what prompts them to start searching for God. Seekers need someone to talk to them. They need to have someone evaluate their beliefs against the standard of Scripture. They need someone to help them construct a new worldview.

A few people are interested enough to ask lots of questions about their Christian friends' faith and come to Christ after straightforward conversations about the gospel. But many are so wrapped up in their own worlds and so content with their current beliefs that they ask few questions. In those cases we must work hard to find points of contact and pray hard that God will break through into their lives.

Where does all this leave us? Jesus has commissioned us to make disciples. To do so we must walk a tightrope between conforming to the world and isolating ourselves from it. The Bible maintains that balance throughout. It engages critically with other worldviews. It affirms the truth in them and denies the error. We need to maintain the same balance. We must know the gospel. We must understand the world in which we live. We must pray and keep on praying. Then God will take our lives, our words, our presentations of the gospel, and our critiques of others' worldviews and, by his Holy Spirit, will do an astonishing work in their lives.

We need to develop the mental tools to help people do what Paul did in Athens, and even to do what the Lord Jesus did when he stepped into human culture in order to redeem human beings. There is a world to be won and most of us need all the help we can get.

PART 3

Working with the world

PHIL WALL

Introduction

NICK POLLARD

When Jesus called the disciples, he invited them to join him, he asked them to be with him. In the years that followed, they lived with him, ate with him and worked with him. They came to feel they belonged with him.

What they didn't do, until rather later, was to understand much of his teaching. This came with time. When Jesus asked Peter, 'Who do you say I am?' Peter replied, 'You are the Christ, the Son of the living God' (Matt. 16:15–16). This was a key point in the life of the disciples: now they not only belonged to Jesus but also believed the truth about him.

Their behaviour still let them down, however. James and John argued about who should sit next to Jesus in glory (Mark 10:37). When Jesus asked the disciples to stay with him while he prayed in the Garden of Gethsemane, they fell asleep. 'The spirit is willing, but the body is weak,' he commented (Mark 14:38). When Jesus was arrested, Peter denied that he knew him, and even called down curses on himself (Mark 14:71). They belonged and believed, but they didn't yet behave terribly well.

We see, then, a sequence in Jesus' call to follow him. First they were called to *belong*; gradually they were able to *believe*, then eventually they *behaved*.

Unfortunately, the church has tended to reverse this sequence. We first ask them to behave in a particular way. They must come to church. They must sit quietly. They must stop doing some things, and start doing others, before they can become disciples of Jesus Christ.

If they manage that, we then try to help them to believe. We communicate information to them through sermons and books. We take them to discussion groups and discipleship classes. We elicit their assent to certain doctrines.

Finally, when they behave in the right way and believe the right things, we might let them feel that they belong.

Why have we turned the biblical pattern on its head? Why do we not follow the way of Jesus?

Partly it is because we feel insecure when people in our group do not conform to group standards. Partly it is because we place too much emphasis on the intellectual aspect of belief. But if we are serious about being biblical Christians and reaching beyond the fringe, we must reverse our sequence of 'behave, believe, belong'. 'Belong, believe, behave' is the biblical order.

Longing to belong

Moreover, this biblical sequence is culturally relevant. In our postmodern world, people are desperately seeking community. Families and other groupings disintegrate around us. Yet we all feel a need to belong.

This is one reason for the success of TV soaps. The communities in Ramsey Street or Emmerdale or Brookside or Albert Square appeal to us because we feel we know them and the intimate lives and relationships of the characters in them.

The French scholar Michael Maffesoli has written of what he calls 'neo-tribalism'. Individuals desperately searching for community group together and sport the symbolic tags of tribal allegiance, such as designer labels or a style of dress. But these neo-tribes are not stable communities like the ancient tribes. Membership is easily revocable, so neo-tribes are always in flux.

Similarly, the British sociologist Zygmunt Bauman writes of communities which exist only in occasional out-bursts of togetherness. Football matches, demonstrations and festivals are imagined communities where we attempt to replace the lost experience of permanent community with temporary community events. Of course, these neo-tribes and imagined communities are deeply unfulfilling.

Jesus came to include the excluded, and we must follow his strategy by offering people the opportunity to be part of our community. Once they feel they belong, we pray that they will come to believe and then to behave appropriately. But it all begins with belonging.

Phil Wall's commitment to biblical models of evangelism has led him to reach beyond the fringe by inviting people to belong. He invites them to join in the work of the kingdom before they share its beliefs or adopt its behaviour.

Working with the world

PHIL WALL

1. Action and involvement

Peter (not his real name) was a businessman who lived in Scotland. He was the brother of a friend of mine who was concerned that he had made no commitment to follow Jesus. I had never met him, and wanted to contact him without making him feel pressured or got at. He was in marketing, and as I was launching a new project I phoned him and booked an appointment to see him next time he was in London. We talked a lot about the project. I sought his advice on many aspects of it, and he offered to help as it developed. Over the next few months I used him as a sounding-board and advisor. Christ featured in our conversations, often in relation to his sister's faith.

We recently met up again to talk further about the project and how I might take it on to the next stage. I wanted to turn the conversation to Christ and to talk more deeply about where he was in regard to faith. As we talked, it quickly became apparent that God had been at work in him. He wanted to talk about Jesus more than about my project. A couple of hours later, after a rich and deep discussion about what it means to follow Christ, we prayed. He became a follower of Jesus, and his life started to change greatly.

Christians have always struggled to reach those outside the church. Each year, new Christian books attempt to isolate the 'one problem' at the heart of this state of affairs. But of course there are many reasons why we struggle to reach not-yet-Christians, and even the best books on evangelism can offer only partial solutions.

It is with this in mind that I want to examine the process of belief. I have become increasingly convinced that many Christians misunderstand the nature of belief. Addressing this issue will not solve all our evangelistic problems, but it may well take us one step closer to getting it right.

Believe to belong, or belong to believe?

For years after I became a Christian, I assumed that belief was the doorway to belonging. The process of discipleship began when people committed themselves to Jesus. The next step was to get involved in the life of the church.

This seemed to make sense for a number of reasons. First, there was no point in going to church if you did not believe the gospel. Since the church was the people of God, what place did unbelievers have there? Secondly, the church had struggled for years because it was full of people who did not really believe the gospel. I figured that if the church wanted to be on fire for God, it needed to ensure that its members believed the right things. If its activities were to be successful, they should be run by Christians who were sold out for God. Otherwise, God would not bless what we did.

This understanding of belief seemed borne out as I read

about the challenge of the gospel to lukewarm believers (Rev. 3:14–20). God wanted his people to start taking belief seriously, I reasoned. The last thing he needed was a church full of people who did not believe even the fundamentals of the gospel.

Over the years I have altered my thinking, although I remain convinced – increasingly so – that what we believe is important. The change has come about as I have reconsidered the role that belonging plays in helping us to form and develop our belief. I used to think that belief was simply about accepting the probable truth of a set of propositions. I now think that belief goes far deeper than that. True belief involves becoming so convinced of the truth of something (or someone) that we are willing to transform our behaviour accordingly. The more we understand Jesus, the deeper our relationship with him will grow, and the more committed we will become to his purposes in the world.

As soon as we take belief seriously, we recognize that we need as much help as possible: 'I do believe; help me overcome my unbelief!' (Mark 9:24). One of the greatest aids to belief is community. It is within community that we flesh out our beliefs. God set apart the nation of Israel to show the other nations what it meant to live as the people of God. It is within community that our questions about faith can begin to be answered by those more experienced than ourselves. It is within community that we find the safe place that we need to work out what we truly believe. For these reasons, belonging to the community of the church is not just an add-on to our beliefs. It is the context in which we are best able to form our beliefs.

Instead of thinking that people must believe before they can belong, therefore I have begun to realize that a better model is to invite people to belong so that they may believe. I am increasingly convinced that the church needs to adjust its understanding of belief in this light.

Whenever I advocate this change, I encounter opposition. It is not difficult to see why. Change is always difficult, especially when it involves things that we have held dear for many years. You may already be feeling angered by the transformation that I am proposing. At the least, you probably have a number of questions and concerns in mind. Before you reject my proposal out of hand, I would ask you to read to the end of the chapter, so that even if you still disagree with me, you may understand a little more of the thinking behind this outlandish suggestion.

The problem of believing before you belong

There are some serious problems with thinking that people must believe before they can belong. Let us look at three.

Problem 1: does it work?

I am a pragmatist by nature. One of the first questions I ask about anything is whether it works. Admittedly, not everything that works is necessarily true, but anything that is true should work.

Insisting that people believe before they can belong does not work. Most of us see few people come to faith. Furthermore, most of us struggle to attract not-yet-Christians to our evangelistic events, let alone to our normal church services. I have spoken at countless evangelistic events which lacked one vital ingredient – someone to evangelize.

The fact that not-yet-Christians are rarely to be found in church, despite the increasing hunger for spirituality that we find all around us, raises some embarrassing questions. In his book *Christian Apologetics in the Postmodern World*, Philip Kenneson challenges our desire to prove the truth of our belief:

> ... what our world is waiting for, and what the church seems reluctant to offer, is not more incessant talk about objective truth, but an embodied witness that clearly demonstrates why anyone should care about any of this in the first place. The fact that most of our non-christian neighbours cannot pick us out from the rest of their non-christian neighbours – or if they can, what makes us pick-outable are matters relatively incidental to the gospel – suggests that they are right in refusing to accept what we *say* we believe but which our *lives* make a lie.

In our society, families are breaking down, the most feared disease is loneliness, and many people spend their lives struggling for acceptance by others. Jesus is the ultimate answer to all these problems. Surely people should be flocking to church to discover him.

They should be, but they are not. Instead, cults and bizarre religious movements see massive growth while the church struggles on. Many cults grow because they are strong where the church is so often weak – in their expression of belonging.

Although many people have a huge hunger for spirituality, they are rarely ready to ask, 'What must I do to be saved?' Most are not even ready to ask basic questions about the nature and purposes of Jesus Christ.

The first question that most people ask is simply, 'Who will support me in my time of need?' 'Who will get alongside me in the midst of my broken relationship?' 'Who will help me to find employment now that I have been sacked?' 'Who will encourage me when I feel depressed?' It is at this level that the church needs to engage with people's needs.

The best way to do this is by encouraging them to become part of a community of people who love them and care for them. The details of the gospel can wait. They are important, but they must take second place to the heart of the gospel – that God loves people. Most are not ready to tackle the big intellectual questions about faith; their immediate focus is on finding somewhere where they can belong. We must adjust our philosophy of mission, which is so often concerned with wanting to prove a point, for in our culture many struggle to accept that there is a point to life that is worth proving.

Since the church continues to lose thousands of people to bizarre cults and empty religions, it must recognize that something is going wrong. We cannot dismiss this phenomenon by asserting that Christianity is not always popular. Too often I have heard Christians reject the need for change by arguing that the way to Christianity is narrow. This often means that their subculture of gospel communication is narrow and costs too much to change. They want to narrow the road of discipleship too quickly. It is after we have passed through the small gate that we set out on the narrow pathway of discipleship (Matt. 7:13–14). We must aim to provide many access points to the one Saviour.

Although what Jesus said was not always popular, he himself was immensely popular among the ordinary people. He had difficulty getting get away from the crowds. Wherever he went, people followed. Even some of the religious leaders, who were the object of Jesus' harshest criticisms, were drawn to him. Read the account of Nicodemus in John 3, 7 and 19.

If the church is to be the body of Christ in this world, we need to rediscover his model of disciple-making. Although our message will not always be popular, people should be attracted to us. Before they are attracted to our words, they will be attracted to our expression of community, for we are the *body* of Christ in this world.

Problem 2: are we consistent?

The second problem with asking people to believe before they can belong is that we apply this model inconsistently, and so appear hypocritical. Any belief that cannot be applied consistently requires re-examination.

Many Christians, for example, would be deeply concerned about allowing a not-yet-Christian to be involved in a dramatic presentation in a church service. Yet they would probably be less concerned if that same not-yet-Christian undertook some building work for their church. We insist that people believe before they belong, yet we would happily employ an atheist to do a job for us.

This distinction involves drawing a divide between the spiritual and the physical. We do not mind who helps us with physical tasks, but we are careful to check the beliefs of anyone involved in 'spiritual' activities. This dualism is a major stumbling-block for the contemporary church. It leads to ignoring large areas of life on the grounds that God is interested only in the spiritual bits. On what basis can we argue that playing in the worship group is more important than cleaning the church toilet? Do we really want to suggest that Jesus went about his Father's business only when he did overtly spiritual acts? If God is so unconcerned with the physical and practical needs of his creation, why did he create it in the first place?

The more we think about it, the more we must see that our division between the spiritual and the physical is entirely unbiblical. The kingdom of God involves both the spiritual and the physical. Jesus preached the good news, but he also fed hungry people and healed sick ones. Those who reject the biblical call to social action on the grounds that they are interested only in winning souls open themselves to the charge of heresy. The overwhelming passion of God for the physical needs and concerns of his creation is evident throughout Scripture. The Pentateuch, the histories, the prophetic and wisdom literature, the Psalms, the life and teaching of Jesus and the writings of the apostles are saturated with it. It is the fact that the gospel is good news for the whole person that makes it so exciting.

Inconsistent beliefs require re-examination because truth is consistent by its very nature. If we want to be consistent, we have two options. Either we reject our 'believe and belong' model, or we employ only Christians to help us with our activities, whether 'spiritual' or 'physical'.

Some Christians have tried to address this inconsistency by going for the second option. When I was in America a few years ago, I came across a *Christian Yellow Pages*, designed to make sure that Christians could employ fellow Christians to meet all their physical needs. I found the idea offensive because it cuts Christians off from the world rather than sending them into it. Anyway, presumably even the users of the *Christian Yellow Pages* don't demand Christian credentials when they have to call the emergency services!

Problem 3: does the Bible back it?

The greatest problem with insisting on belief before belonging is that it has little biblical precedent.

Look at the model of evangelism used by Jesus. When he met the woman at the well, he related to her in a positive manner. There were at least three good reasons why, in his culture, he should never have spoken to her at all. First, she was a woman. Secondly, she was an immoral woman, and thirdly, she was an immoral Samaritan woman (a race despised by the Jews).

Despite these barriers, Jesus built a relationship with her. He actually asked her for help. This is amazing given his supernatural knowledge about her lifestyle. What might we have said to her? Given her a three-point sermon? I doubt if we would have asked her for help, but that is precisely the strategy that Jesus adopted: 'Will you give me a drink?' (John 4:8).

Here we have Jesus, morally perfect, God incarnate, inviting a 'loose woman' (who had probably spent most of her life being abused by men) to draw water for him from the well. She subsequently believed, and told those around her: 'Come, see a man who told me everything I ever did. Could this be the Christ?' (4:29). The disciples were surprised by Jesus' actions (4:27). They had to accept the fact that God had a different way of doing things. Could it be that our negative response to the idea of not-yet-Christians beginning by belonging is like the surprise of the early disciples, rooted in prejudice?

The story of the woman at the well was the norm rather than the exception. Jesus did not select his disciples on the basis of their theological understanding. They continually failed to recognize who he was and what he had come to do. Nor did he begin by asking them to sign a statement of belief. He did not even take them through a copy of *Journey into Life*! Why? It was not because he thought belief unimportant. The opposite was the case. Jesus knew more than anyone else just how important belief was, and much of his time was spent teaching the disciples. He also knew that the best way to help people to believe is to allow them to belong. The disciples came to belief by belonging to a distinct community. Their Christianity was both 'taught' and 'caught' as they spent time with Jesus, listening, observing and acting. They tasted truth in him, and it was belonging that drew them to faith. Their belief was not the doorway to belonging; it was the fruit of it.

Consider how Jesus called Peter to follow him (Mark 1:16–18). Did he ask Peter to believe before belonging (model 1) or to belong before believing (model 2)? Using model 1, Jesus would have said something like the following: 'Listen, Peter. Take this copy of the Old Testament, and when you have worked out that I am the Messiah, pray the sinner's prayer and follow me.'

Using model 2, he would have said something like the following: 'Listen, Peter. Why don't you come and hang out with me for a while, observe what I do, listen to what I say, and even get involved and do some of the things that I do? Then you will come to understand who I am and what I am about.' It does not take a theological genius to work out which model Jesus chose to use.

Every time I read the Gospels, I am challenged by the way Jesus empowered his disciples to get involved in the work of the kingdom. In Mark 6:7–13 he sent out the twelve disciples to preach and cast out demons, *before* he asked them whether or not they understood who he was (Mark 8:27–33). (The same order is followed in Luke 9:1–6; 9:18–22, and Matthew 10:1–42; 16:13–20.) We, by contrast, insist that people can really get involved only after they have understood who Jesus is and what he came to do. I am not suggesting that we invite seekers or brand-new believers to preach (though God has often used their questions and testimonies to teach 'the flock' powerful lessons). What I am saying is that we need to risk involving people so that they may belong.

The roots of our confusion

Why have we misunderstood the process of disciple-making so badly? Four factors contribute to our confusion.

1. Isolationism

Many churches want nothing to do with the world. They believe that to be involved with the world is to compromise their holiness. At its most extreme, isolationism results in monasteries and convents that cut themselves off from contact with the world. Didn't God call Israel to be a separate and holy nation?

It is true that God called Israel to be a separate and holy nation, but we must not forget his missionary purpose in doing so. Consider the geographical location of Israel. God placed Israel among other nations. If he had wanted to cut them off from the world, the island of Cyprus would have been a more sensible location. God called Israel to show the pagan nations what it meant to live as the people of God. He called them to live differently so that others might see how to live.

Similarly, God calls the church to be salt and light in this world (Matt. 5:13–16). As Cardinal Suhard reminds us: 'To be a witness does not consist in engaging in propaganda, nor even in stirring people up, but in being a living mystery. It means to live in such a way that one's life would not make sense if God did not exist' (Timothy P. Phillips, *Clinton Apologizes in the Postmodern World*, IVP USA). We are to be living contradictions: to live differently from the nations while remaining involved in their world, so that we may influence them for Jesus.

Much of the isolationism of contemporary evangelicalism can be traced back to the Puritans. Puritans reacted against the corruption in the church of their day. Attempting to rediscover the distinctiveness of Christianity, they formed communities that shied away from contact with the rest of the world. The Puritans emphasized the distinctiveness of Christianity and, in so doing, rejected many aspects of their culture, such as theatre and dance. While their intentions were good – to protect the purity of the church – this aspect of their legacy has been unhelpful. A spirit of isolationism runs counter to the strategy of Jesus, who became one of us in our world.

One of the most amazing passages in Scripture tells us that 'The Word became flesh and made his dwelling among us' (John 1:14). In this statement, John establishes God's strategy for reaching his creation – the incarnation of his Son. When Jesus entered into the world, he showed us what real holiness is all about. Holiness does not involve staying away from everything sinful. Had that been the case, God would not have come near our fallen world. Jesus entered our world so that it might come to understand the holiness of God. Biblical holiness is linked to redemption.

Incarnational evangelism raises the problem of how we can be in the world and yet not of it (John 17:14–18). Holiness means to be 'set apart' in the way God is set apart: we are called to be morally and ethically *distinct* but culturally *engaged*. Tragically, the church has often been morally and ethically *indistinct*, but culturally *disengaged*.

Incarnation means 'God with skin on', and, as the body of Christ, that is what we are meant to be. We are *both* to have nothing to do with the world *and* to be totally immersed in it, so that we might transform it. We are not to love the world, yet we must lay down our lives for it. Publicity for the movie *Deep Impact* carried the line: 'When heaven and earth collide.' Heaven collides with earth when the Holy Spirit indwells and works through God's people in the world.

The challenge to our disciple-making is clear. If we are to be imitators of God (Eph. 5:1), we should adopt his method of evangelism. Getting involved in the lives of not-yet-Christians means sharing our lives with them, allowing them to spend time with us just as Jesus allowed sinners to spend time with him. Living holy lives is important, but we are to do so in the midst of a sinful world. If we don't, we fail to understand God's call. We are called to 'incarnate' holiness, not to isolate it.

2. Individualism

A second factor in the church's failure correctly to understand the process of coming to believe is *individualism* – not individuality (expressing our distinctive personalities), but our tendency to focus on the individual at the expense of the wider church community. Many Christians think of faith purely as a relationship between God and an individual. Of course, a personal relationship with God is foundational. But each Christian is *ipso facto* a part of the body of Christ (1 Cor. 12:12–26). God calls us to be get involved in church and to live out our individual relationship with God in community.

One of the big questions used to be whether one had to go to church to be a Christian. This indicates a faith riddled with individualism. Although I no longer hear questions like this in churches I visit, other traces of individualism remain. For example, many Christians still react negatively to the idea of accountability. They do not see why someone else should interfere in matters that are between them and God. This is to misunderstand accountability. Rightly exercised, it means not the assumption of power by a few but the willing subjection to scrutiny of all. One aspect of this is God's teaching about how we should deal with our sin: 'Therefore confess your sins to each other and pray for each other so that you may be healed' (James 5:16a).

Individualism encourages us to think that personal belief is the only thing that matters, and that the church community has no bearing on our individual relationship with God. The result is that we end up belonging to a church because we have to, not because we see any value in it. If we cannot see the value of community in our own relationship with God, it is hardly surprising that we struggle to see its value for not-yet-Christians. Thus we fail to see belonging as foundational in our evangelism.

How did individualism become rife within the church? Because it is rife outside the church. Paul tells us: 'Do not conform any longer to the pattern of this world, but be transformed by the renewing of your mind' (Rom. 12:2). But we regularly fall short of this ideal and are easily influenced by the world around us. Individualism flourished during the Thatcherism of the 1980s. The emphasis was on 'looking after number one', and community was sacrificed at the altar of selfish individualism. This attitude has persisted despite a backlash in recent years.

A further reason for the individualism prevalent in

today's church can be traced back to the birth of Protestantism. In response to the corruption and abuse of power in the Catholic Church at that time, the Reformers emphasized the importance of our individual relationship with God. They reminded us that every individual had direct access to God through Jesus, a doctrine that we term the 'priesthood of all believers'. We do not need priests and saints as intermediaries. While this emphasis was one of the greatest strengths of the Reformation, however, it was to degenerate into one of the greatest weaknesses of Protestantism. The importance of the individual came to be emphasized at the expense of community rather than in the context of community.

3. Instantaneous conversion

Evangelicals are often more concerned with the moment of conversion than with the process of conversion. I have been guilty of this in my own evangelistic preaching, when I have held the gospel up as a 'yes or no', 'in or out', 'now or never' affair. I fear that in my naïve zeal, I may have shut the door to faith for people who, with integrity, were unable to make a decision there and then. I may have misled those who were genuinely seeking after God.

The Bible tells us that salvation is both an event and a process. Jesus saw the new birth as an event (John 3:1–8). Being born again involves making a decision to follow Jesus. This is the point that Jesus is making when he calls us to repent and believe the good news. For evangelicals, this is familiar territory. Our evangelism focuses on calling people to make a decision for Jesus.

Salvation is also a process, however (an idea we may be less comfortable with). As Paul writes: 'Therefore, my dear friends, as you have always obeyed – not only in my presence, but now much more in my absence – continue to work out your salvation with fear and trembling, for it is God who works in you to will and to act according to his good purpose' (Phil. 2:12–13).

Many evangelicals interpret this 'working out' as sanctification rather than as justification. Justification happens when Jesus saves me from my sin and I become a Christian. Sanctification is the next step, whereby I become more and more like Jesus. Both elements are important, but evangelicals often claim that salvation involves only the first element. Yet the Bible integrates the two in a way that makes them difficult to separate. This explains the difficulty we have in trying to locate the exact point of the disciples' conversion. Perhaps it was when they first followed Jesus. Or maybe it was when they preached and healed the sick. We might argue that it was not until they recognized who Jesus was. Or we might maintain that it was not until Jesus had died and risen from the dead, for they did not really appreciate his purposes until then (see John 20:9).

As we get to grips with the Gospel accounts, we find remarkably little evidence that conversion is instant. Instead, the focus is on the idea of conversion as a journey. When I preach at evangelistic meetings these days, I often begin by stating that every human being is on a journey. But where are we, and what should our next step be? These questions are as valid for Buddhists as they are for Baptists, for Sikhs as for Salvationists, and for Muslims as for Methodists. All of us, even the most staunch atheists, are on a spiritual journey.

The description of salvation as a process or journey certainly makes sense of the experiences of a large number of people. For every classic conversion story in which someone can name the moment of salvation, there are scores of individuals who struggle to identify the exact point at which they were converted.

As soon as we recognize that faith is a journey, we can begin to appreciate the importance of other people in helping us to go forward. This is how Jesus helped the first disciples. He called them to journey together with him, and they worked out their beliefs in this context. Belonging comes before belief, for it was after the disciples began to spend time with Jesus that they grew to understand who he was and what he was about.

4. Insecurity

At the heart of our evangelical subculture is a form of insecurity, although we may try to hide it, or dress it up with impressive theological formulas. The real reason we discourage not-yet-Christians from belonging is that we lack confidence in the God who saves. We fear that not-yet-Christians might start to lead the people of God astray if they spend too much time with us. Many of us are so afraid of other worldviews that we seek to keep them at arm's length.

Yet, if Jesus really is the light of the world, he will shine brightest in the spiritual darkness that encompasses our society. Sometimes when I am speaking to students, I invite them to join me in placing all our different perspectives on the table. We can then stand back and see which ones shines the brightest. If Jesus is all that we claim him to be, he will shine brighter than every alternative. When Jesus is placed alongside the legalism of Islam, the hopelessness of atheism, the pointlessness of Buddhism, or the confusion of New Age teaching, there can be no contest. We should be more confident in working alongside those who believe something different, for, as we talk, they will come to see the one who is the way, the truth and the life (John 14:6).

Overcoming the problem

If we accept that belonging often comes before believing, how should we change the way we do evangelism? Change has to begin by assessing the current situation. We need to begin by auditing our church activities and thinking how far they enable people to belong.

Use the table overleaf to see how much of your church programme is accessible to not-yet-Christians. 'Accessible' activities are those at which not-yet-Christians can feel relaxed, and not excluded by obscure liturgies, religious language, dress codes or subtle messages that 'we belong and you don't'. List the activities that are at the centre of your church life, not directly evangelistic events. Be honest. If you think that an activity is accessible to not-yet-Christians, but no not-yet-Christians have attended in the last ten years, the access is probably not as good as you think. I have inserted a couple of activities as examples. If they are not relevant to your church, ignore them.

If your church is like the majority that I spend time in, you may well find there are surprisingly few activities accessible for not-yet-Christians. It is easy to respond by pointing to the church's evangelistic activities. While these are important, however, helping people to belong involves more than putting on an event for them to attend. It requires us to develop activities which they can get involved in. One of the most powerful ways to give people ownership of a group and a strong sense of belonging to it is to give them a role in it. Encouraging people to get involved in our activities is an effective means of encouraging people to begin their journey of faith by belonging.

	CHURCH ACTIVITY	NO ACCESS	LIMITED ACCESS	GOOD ACCESS
		(Please tick one)		
1	Housegroup			
2	Worship group			
3				
4				
5				
6				
7				
8				
9				
10				
11				
12				
13				
14				

The phrase 'Can you help me, please?' is one of the most powerful evangelistic phrases that we can utter. It worked for Jesus with the woman at the well, and it will also work for us.

A good illustration of this comes from my home church. While doing some door-to-door visitation, a member of our church met a man who made and sold drum kits for a living. He also played a mean jazz drum set, and had played with some high-profile jazz bands. When this was reported back to the church, we invited him to help us by drumming at an event we were running. He accepted the invitation and soon became a regular fixture in our worship group, playing drums in church on Sunday mornings. It was about a year later that he committed his life to Christ. His journey to living faith resulted from his involvement with us, including many conversations and a strong sense of belonging.

There are hundreds of ways in which we can enable not-yet-Christians to get involved in our church activities. By doing so we demonstrate trust, belief and genuine interest in them. We could invite them to contribute their time and energy, or their specialist skills. I have suggested ten possibilities below, some fairly simple, others more demanding.

1. Invite a local GP to address a parenting course run at your church.
2. As a church, join others in a practical community scheme. One church that I know of asked local residents to help them paint a pedestrian tunnel that had become an eyesore.
3. Ask friends to help you deliver leaflets advertising church events. A friend of mine who was at university managed to convince his not-yet-Christian friends to

help him deliver evangelistic flyers advertising a mission that the Christian Union was organizing.

4. Invite not-yet-Christians involved in community service to be interviewed in church. For example, you could invite your local MP or councillor to explain his or her work to your church.

5. A great way of challenging people to reconsider their beliefs is to ask them to work alongside us in social-action programmes. For example, consider inviting not-yet-Christians to help you with a soup run for the homeless.

6. Invite not-yet-Christians to advise you on the best way to advertise evangelistic events. Who better to tell you what might attract your target group(s)?

7. If you are preparing a talk for your church, think about asking a not-yet-Christian friend to listen to a practice run and offer comments.

8. How about inviting not-yet-Christian musicians to help out with the music group? Some Christians may object, as though it would mar the sacrifice of worship offered to God. We are often inconsistent, though, when it comes to worship. We do not usually protest if a not-yet-Christian attends our worship service and sings the songs. Why do we think that God is more concerned about a guitar than about a voice?

9. Church leaders could ask a friend who is a management consultant to advise the leadership team on the best way to implement some of its ideas.

10. Why not allow some not-yet-Christians to come along and help with the summer play-scheme? As they hang around with Christians, and help as biblical truths are taught to children, they will probably start to think about Jesus far more than they would do otherwise.

These ideas merely scratch the surface. I hope you are already beginning to think about other possibilities. These ventures involve an element of risk, but surely the eternal lives of men and women are worth it. It is a risk that Jesus was willing to die for.

Linda is a good example of the sort of risk that is worth taking when we encourage not-yet Christians to help the church with specialist skills. She worked as a school cook and was looking to move on when she heard that the local Salvation Army Corps and community centre required a cook. After some initial reluctance, she decided to apply for the post, and got the job.

After a few months of working alongside believers in this environment, Linda was impressed by their lives and decided to accept their invitation to a Sunday service. She was so struck by the service that she brought other members of her family. First came her husband, then her two daughters, then the boyfriend of one daughter, and finally her son. Eventually, she decided to become a Christian. One of her daughters asked to be married in the church, and members of her family continue to attend occasionally.

We often shy away from employing people who are not committed believers. Sometimes there are good reasons for doing so, as we shall go on to consider. But we often make these decisions because we are afraid of allowing outsiders to turn the spotlight on our church community. We mustn't be. 'You are the light of the world. A city on a hill cannot be hidden. Neither do people light a lamp and put it under a bowl. Instead they put it on its stand, and it gives light to everyone in the house. In the same way, let your light shine before others, that they may see your good deeds and praise your Father in heaven' (Matt. 5:14–16).

Recognizing the limitations

Whenever the church strives to engage in mission, it takes a risk. This is unavoidable. Nevertheless, we must use our common sense. Although belonging precedes belief, this model has limitations.

First, not-yet-Christians cannot get involved to the point of sharing in the leadership of God's people. Paul makes it clear that leaders must fulfil certain criteria (1 Tim. 3:1–16). Asking people to lead your church, however, is not the same as asking them to advise your church, as you can always choose to reject the advice if it is not appropriate.

For example, we could not ask a not-yet-Christian to join the leadership team of a new church we hoped to plant, but we could ask a not-yet-Christian in the local community to advise us about that community. The decision on how to use the advice would rest with the leadership team.

Secondly, not-yet-Christians are not equipped to participate in activities which require the Spirit's power. For example, it would not be appropriate for a not-yet-Christian to take part in deliverance ministry, because this requires us to take authority over evil spirits. This authority is given to everyone who becomes a Christian.

But what about the occasion we looked at earlier, when Jesus sent the disciples to cast out demons? They were not really believers at that stage – at least, not in the way that we understand the term. However, Jesus gave them specific authority to cast out demons (Mark 6:7), which enabled them to complete the job they were given.

We all rely on the grace of God to enable us to do the things that we do. God has made me an evangelist, and yet I can fulfil that role successfully only by his grace. Does this mean that I am not qualified to do the job that I do? No. I am simply suggesting that whenever we ask someone (believer or otherwise) to do a particular job, we have to make a common-sense decision whether he or she has the basic ability to do that job.

Although not-yet-Christians can do only what they are equipped to do, there are often ways of involving them nevertheless. Earlier, I suggested inviting not-yet-Christians to help distribute evangelistic leaflets advertising a forthcoming mission. When my friend tried to do this at his university, he was told by some members of the Christian Union that not-yet-Christians were not equipped for this role. What would happen if someone began to ask the not-yet-Christian questions about Christianity?

My friend's response was twofold. First, so what? It was hardly likely to do a great deal of harm if two not-yet-Christians got talking about questions of faith. In their confusion, they were more likely to want to come along to the mission and get some answers! The second part of my friend's response offered a possible solution. How about a not-yet-Christian working alongside a believer in delivering evangelistic leaflets? This provided a means by which the not-yet-Christian could be better equipped to do the job he or she had been asked to do. If someone began asking questions about Jesus, the believer could explain things to both the not-yet-Christians.

Conclusion

After finishing her accountancy exams, Carol began work in a successful accountancy firm. Things appeared to be going well. As time went by, however, Carol felt increasingly dissatisfied with the job she was doing. As a result, she decided to write to the Salvation Army to offer her assistance for one night a week in any social or community programmes they were running. Carol's offer was accepted, and she was soon involved with others in a project to renovate a run-down council flat that was due to be given to a homeless family.

As she worked alongside Christians, friendships were built. It was not long before Carol, who had previously attended church irregularly, chose to attend regularly with her new friends. She quickly became part of this church community, and subsequently accepted an invitation to join an Alpha course. The result was that she committed her life to Christ and became a member of the Christian community. Soon after that, Carol decided to leave her well-paid job in the accountancy firm and become the finance officer for a community-based nursery.

Our world is full of people like Carol who would be far more open to belief if only they could begin by belonging. In view of this, we really must be a church where people can begin their spiritual journeys by belonging. A good friend of mine says that church should be a place where Jesus feels at home. When we read the Gospel accounts, we cannot fail to see that belief would not be a precondition for belonging to such a place. Recognizing this has huge ramifications for our approach to mission. Instead of concentrating our evangelism on preaching to strangers, we need to begin by enabling people to see who and what we are. This is the missionary strategy of those who understand the true nature of belief. This is the approach to mission adopted by Jesus.

In the strength you have

NICK POLLARD

We have come a long way since chapter 1 of this book. We have looked in detail at three ways in which we can reach out beyond the fringe. My friends have written in an exciting and inspiring way. You may feel ready to get up and go.

Or perhaps despite all you have learned through this book, you may feel inadequate and incapable. If so, welcome to the club! I do as well. And we are in good company: Gideon felt the same way too!

Remember where we left off. Gideon had been told by an angel to 'Go …' But he added: '… in the strength you have' (Judg. 6:14).

If we want to learn from the life of Gideon and to apply this command to ourselves, it is important to hear God's qualification of the command to 'go'. He calls us to go in the strength we have, not to wait until we have some extra ability, power or knowledge. Many of us feel we are not good enough to be involved in evangelism, so we don't do it. We assume it is a task for others who are better at it.

Sometimes this feeling of impotence comes from having picked up the wrong model of evangelism. We might be tempted to think that evangelism is done by people who are, as it were, on the top of a hill. They haven't got any doubts. They never really sin. They are wonderful, godly people – super-Christians, in fact. According to this model, evangelism means that the people on the top of the hill throw a rope down to the poor sinners at the bottom, saying, 'Grab hold of this rope and we'll pull you up so that you can be like us.'

Of course that's wrong. Rather, evangelism leads us, with our faults, failings, doubts and fears, to walk with non-Christians at the foot of the mountain, pointing to Jesus who is on the top. It means saying, 'Won't you join us as we walk together to become more like Jesus?'

God uses as he chooses

I often find it hard to believe that God could ever use someone like me to bring others to faith in him. When I get to know other evangelists well, I find that they feel the same. People who don't know us aren't aware of our weaknesses and faults and failings. But they are very real. And yet God chooses to use us! Sometimes I catch myself even wondering if God knows what I am really like. But that is ridiculous. God sees right through me – and yet he chooses to use me.

The fact is that God uses us because he has chosen to do so, not as a reward for our achievement. He doesn't use us because of what we are like, but despite what we are like.

Sometimes I look around at the people in church. These are the people whom God has chosen to change this world. I don't know what your church is like, but if you were going to choose a group of people to change the world, would you choose that lot? Probably not. There is dear old Mrs Smith, who plays the organ and dribbles. And there is the vicar, who is trying so hard to be a wit – and he's halfway there. These are not the kind of people that we would choose to change the world. But they are the people God has chosen. They are people like you and me, with all our faults and failings.

I can't tell you how many times I have sat and thought, 'I can't go on as an evangelist any more.' I often feel like giving up. I am only too aware of my own weaknesses and inadequacies. Yet God chooses to use me, just as he wants to use every Christian – and as he chose to use Gideon.

Gideon too felt completely inadequate for the task that God had given him. When God called him to go, he protested: 'But Lord, how can I save Israel? My clan is the weakest in Manasseh, and I am the least in my family' (Judg. 6:15).

Centuries before, Jacob (the son of Isaac, who was the son of Abraham) also had a close encounter with God. The Bible records how God wrestled and struggled with him all night (Gen. 32:24). God spoke to him and changed his name to Israel, which means 'struggled'.

Israel had twelve sons. From eleven of them, eleven of the twelve tribes of Israel were descended. But one of the sons, the boy called Joseph, became unpopular with his brothers. Consumed with jealousy, they plotted against him and sold him into slavery. He ended up in Egypt, where eventually he had two sons, whom he called Ephraim and Manasseh.

In due course, Joseph's father and brothers were reconciled with him in Egypt, and Israel adopted Joseph's sons as his own. But when he laid hands on them to bless them, he crossed his arms. Consequently Ephraim, the younger son, got the right hand of blessing (that is, the stronger blessing, normally bestowed on the eldest son), while Manasseh, the older son, got the left hand. The people of Manasseh, therefore, were considered not only a 'half-tribe', but the weaker half-tribe at that.

Manasseh was Gideon's tribe. Furthermore, his clan was the weakest within it. And he was the least in his family. In effect, he told God, 'You can't get smaller than me, Lord! You've really picked a good one here, haven't you?'

Gideon didn't have much self-esteem or a good self-image. He was probably born apologizing to the midwife for taking up so much of her time.

But how does the Lord reply? He doesn't say, 'I hadn't realized that. No, you are not good enough to serve me.' Nor does he invite Gideon to take time out for in-depth counselling. He doesn't take him back over his early life experiences with a view to boosting his self-image. He simply tells him, 'I will be with you' (verse 16).

It seems that having the Lord with him is all that Gideon needs. He doesn't need more strength or more ability. He is told to go in the strength he has.

We are in much the same situation today. If we are Christians, the Lord is with us, and he calls us to go in the strength we have.

Sometimes we are tempted to believe that we can't start reaching those beyond the fringe until we have sorted out our own lives. But on that basis we would never obey God's command. We will never have our lives sorted out this side of heaven.

This temptation often derives from a misunderstanding of Jesus' words to the disciples in Acts 1:4. He told them not to leave Jerusalem to evangelize until they had received the gift that his Father had promised: the Holy Spirit.

They obeyed Jesus and waited. On the day of Pentecost, God's Holy Spirit came to them and they were able to go out in power. Three thousand people became Christians that day.

We are living after Pentecost. We no longer have to wait for God to send his Spirit upon us. If we are Christians, God's Holy Spirit has already come into our lives. We don't have to wait for another Pentecost until we are ready to go out. But we do need to get up and go.

Of course, that doesn't make it easy. Evangelism never is; that's why I called my first book *Evangelism Made Slightly Less Difficult*. The Bible promises that we will suffer and struggle. Paul says, 'To this end I labour, struggling with all his energy which so powerfully works in me' (Col. 1:9). But as we do so, we will experience God's energy working powerfully in us too.

Throughout the Bible we can see that people who sought to live for God struggled. Indeed, as we saw a few pages ago, the very name Israel means 'struggled'. The children of Israel knew they were children of struggle.

That goes for us too. But if we won't labour and struggle, if we won't go in the strength we have, knowing that God is with us, we will never reach those who are beyond the fringe.

269.2
P772B

LINCOLN CHRISTIAN COLLEGE AND SEMINARY

99345

3 4711 00152 9884